THE ALTERNATIVE HOLIDAY GUIDE TO

Exploring Nature in North Africa

by

Robert Chote

and

Julian Cremona

Ashford
Southampton
1989

Published by Ashford
            1 Church Road,
            Shedfield,
            Hampshire.
            SO3 2HW

British Library Cataloguing in Publication Data

Cremona, Julian
 The alternative holiday guide to exploring nature in North Africa.
 1. Africa. North Africa. Natural history.
 Activities.
 I. Title II. Chote, Robert
 508.61

 ISBN 1–85253–161–4

Designed and typeset by Jordan and Jordan, Fareham, Hampshire

Printed in Great Britain by BPCC Wheatons Ltd, Exeter

While great care has been taken in the compilation of this book, the author
and publisher cannot guarantee that all details, such as prices, schedules,
addresses and telephone numbers will remain unchanged and exactly as
quoted here.
    The authors have no connection with any business or establishment
cited here, and no guarantee or endorsement is implied or given in this
respect. That a business or establishment is *not* listed or detailed does not
imply any criticism.

Contents

Introduction to North Africa

Planning and Preparation

Morocco

Algeria

Tunisia

List of Maps

List of Photographs

Preface

Tunisia, Morocco and Algeria, the three north African countries discussed in this book, offer ideal destinations for a range of different travellers. Primarily this includes the growing numbers of people who want to explore further afield than the common 'tourist-package' holiday resorts. You may be an independent backpacker, a group in a minibus, travelling on your own or with friends or as a family; you may be an organiser of a school group, or a longer-term traveller. In addition it is hoped that the book will appeal to everyone who appreciates the natural world. In an era of package deals and 'all-inclusion', more and more people are choosing to travel independently. Moreover, many people are beginning to look beyond the confines of Europe, to find something a little out of the ordinary. Even so, those who opt for the package holiday will still find plenty in the book to enrich their experience.

Tunisia is perhaps the closest to a 'holiday' destination. It lacks the grinding urban and rural poverty that the other nations suffer. An excellent network of public buses means that the lone backpacker is able to cover much of the country in a relatively short period of time. Similarly, there are few areas that cannot be reached with a standard family car. This convenience has its drawback in the growth of the 'package-deal' tourist trade. Nonetheless, the country boasts an interesting natural history, with attractive cities and diverse landscapes.

At the other extreme, Algeria is not an easy country to visit. There is little point in going there without your own vehicle. It is, though, accessible to a well-organised youth or school group, or to an expedition of five or six members. The rewards for overcoming adversity, however, are considerable. A visit to Algeria is certainly an adventure.

Morocco strikes a happy medium. You can see a good deal of the country by relying on public transport. With a reasonably robust vehicle, though, you can move from the remarkable imperial cities to spectacular gorges or classic sand-dune desert scenery.

To prepare the ground for the country-by-country chapters, we have included a section that provides a general introduction to north Africa. It discusses the geography and natural history of the region as a whole. On a more practical level, the 'Planning and Preparation' section draws on our own experiences. It deals with a range of topics, including culture shock, vehicles, off-road driving techniques, camping, hotels, food, clothing, money, photography and health problems. A checklist of medical supplies and vehicle spares is provided at the end.

The main part of *Exploring Nature in North Africa* is a series of three routes. We do not pretend to provide an exhaustive guide. Instead, we offer a single journey through each country, which we have found to encompass much of the variety and flavour which that country offers. Where a number of interesting alternatives exist, we try to describe them in full. Consequently, you may not easily be able to visit all the places we describe in the course of a single tour.

As we lay considerable emphasis on the botanical, zoological and geographical interest of the places we describe, we have not attempted comprehensive descriptions of the towns on our routes. We have, though, attempted to provide a taste of what they offer, suggesting one or two of the principal sights that a visitor with limited time might wish to see.

The descriptive chapters on Morocco, Algeria and Tunisia will be useful at two stages of planning. First, by reading all three, you will be able to decide which country suits you best, both in terms of what it offers, and what resources you have available. Second, having selected your destination, the detailed route will provide an excellent basis around which to plan your itinerary. You will have to accept some inaccuracy as this book dates with time – flash floods and the break-up of desert roads may cause some problems. As bureaucracy is a constant concern of the traveller in Africa, you should contact the Tourist Office in London before departure in order to learn of any changes in the documentation.

Ultimately, our hope in writing this book is to inspire you to discover the beauty and fascination of north Africa for yourself. It is not as inaccessible as you may think, and having visited only once, you may never be satisfied by lazing on a beach again!

Acknowledgements

This book originated from an expedition to Morocco in 1985. As with the journeys that inspired our previous book, *Exploring Nature in the Wilds of Europe*, this expedition involved the students and staff of St Mary's College in Southampton. To all those who took part or helped in any way, we offer our gratitude.

Algeria is a vast and changing country. We owe much to recent explorers, Richard Deverell and Adrian Board, who have helped considerably in the organisation of the section on Algeria. Both had travelled on St Mary's College expeditions, and since then have used their experience to mount more ambitious projects. Adrian journeyed southwards from Tamanrasset to Cameroon. Richard made his way westwards into Mali, to carry out six weeks' work for Intermediate Technology. On his return he crossed the dangerous Tanezrouft sands to Bechar. Both have allowed us to use some of their photographs in this book.

All the tourist offices in London were very helpful. We must, though, extend our particular thanks to Rachid Mardassi of the Tunisian Tourist Board. Joan Holt and Phil Read have each accompanied one of our journeys to Tunisia, and we are grateful for their useful observations.

Identification of species found in north Africa has always been a problem. Simon Reavey's entomological skills have helped considerably over the years and, before we set off for Morocco in 1985, Dr John Larmuth of Cambridge University gave us a great deal of helpful advice.

Dr John Elliot has continued to support our expeditions through the years by helping with health matters. He has also produced the breakdown of medical problems in the 'Planning and Preparation' section. Similarly, Merry Oak Spares and Brooklyn Engineering, both in the Southampton area, have given their expertise in the supply of spare parts and knowledge (vehicular rather than anatomical!). They have also helped produce the checklist of vehicle parts. The preparation and repair of our ageing vehicles has been undertaken by Bill Parsons of Rapidgrove Ltd, also in Southampton. He must surely dread the return of our Land Rovers each year!

Since the first expedition in 1975, Brenda Cremona has provided crucial support as Deputy Leader. She has made valuable comments in the preparation of this book, as well as drawing the maps.

Finally, thanks to Kathryn Robinson, who mercilessly exposed some of the more outrageous deficiencies in our prose style. Her criticisms were, as always, harsh but fair. The blame for what remains, however, lies squarely with the authors.

Robert Chote,
Queens' College, Cambridge

Julian Cremona,
St Mary's College, Southampton

October 1988

INTRODUCTION TO NORTH AFRICA

The Tizi-n-Tichka pass through the High Atlas

Geography

As a result of the movement of the world's crustal plates, Africa has steadily drifted northwards, colliding with Europe. Consequently, the sea between Spain and Morocco – the Straits of Gibraltar – is only a few kilometres wide at this point. The immense pressure of this collision has produced folds in the earth's crust. These folds are the Sierra Nevada mountains in Spain and the Atlas mountains in Morocco. The Atlas is a compound of ranges: the Rif, the Middle Atlas, the High Atlas and the Saharan Atlas.

The Rif mountains are near the coast. Further inland, the Middle Atlas rise to an altitude of 3,000 m. Beyond a plain to the south, the High Atlas reach nearly 5,000 m. The Saharan Atlas, a smaller range which stands on the fringe of the desert, is almost devoid of life because of the arid conditions. The Atlas ranges are not confined to Morocco. They extend across to Tunisia, where their height has lessened so much that they are merely hills and no longer discernible as separate ranges.

These fold mountains all lie to the north of a line stretching from Agadir in Morocco to southern Tunisia. This block of land has itself become separated from the rest of north Africa by a series of major fault and fracture lines. Much of this rock is sedimentary, although volcanic rock has broken through in the western parts of the High Atlas, where a number of extinct volcanoes can be seen. Plate tectonics – the movement of one continent relative to another – inevitably causes cracks in the earth's crust. As a result, earthquakes and volcanoes are common. Over the years, a number of devastating earthquakes have rocked Algeria. The Hoggar region, to the east of Tamanrasset in the south of the country, is the most dramatic volcanic region in north Africa. Huge volcanic plugs dominate the landscape. Some of the rocks here are among the oldest known on earth.

The plains to the south of the Atlas ranges were once below sea level. Although the land has risen considerably since that time, these plains can almost be recognised as a long lost part of the Mediterranean. This **chott** landscape is desolate but dramatically unusual. After the winter rains, large shallow lakes develop. A high concentration of salt means that very little animal or plant life can survive. In the summer, the lakes dry up, leaving cracked mud and a salt crust. The chotts are typical of Algeria and Tunisia, where the land is not very steep. Saline conditions are not just associated with the chotts. As water evaporates from the soil, so minerals are brought to the surface. In temperate regions, salt is washed away from the soil, while in hotter conditions it accumulates.

Desert landscapes vary considerably. Three main types exist in the Sahara. Sand dunes, called **ergs**, occupy barely a fifth of the Sahara's area. Of the different types of dune, the most common in north Africa is the **barchan**. These mobile crescents can form hills over 100 m in height. Most of the desert is a coarse, flat plateau of pebbles. This is referred to as **hamada**. Over the centuries, the pebbles break down into a fine gravel, known as **reg**. Combinations of all three types can be found.

Climate

The worldwide distribution of deserts is far from random. They are found in areas just to the north and south of the equator, bisected by the Tropics of Cancer and Capricorn. The winds blowing south to the Sahara cross the narrow Mediterranean Sea. Consequently, they contain little moisture. Any clouds that do gather disappear as they hit the barrier of the Atlas. The mountains act as a rain shadow, ensuring arid conditions to the south by preventing the movement of water.

Changes in air pressure occasionally produce dust storms. These are followed by squalls of rain which result from the condensation of moisture. Dust storms are commonest in the southern Sahara.

Desert temperatures are moderate in winter (you may need a thin pullover during the day). Nights are cold. During the summer, daytime temperatures exceed 40°C (104°F) while nights are pleasantly warm.

Mean daily maximum and minimum temperatures, in degrees Centigrade

	January max.	min.	April max.	min.	July max.	min.	October max.	min.
Casablanca	17	8	21	11	26	19	24	15
Tamanrasset	19	4	30	13	34	22	29	15
Tunis (average)	– 11 –		– 16 –		– 26 –		– 20 –	

Humidity is low, except in some coastal regions. This makes the heat more tolerable. In dry heat of 40°C (104°F) the body's cooling system can operate effectively as long as you top up lost water at regular intervals. If you put your fingers on the bulb of a thermometer, the mercury column drops as your sweat cools it.

Vegetation

Three main zones of vegetation can be distinguished as you move south. The coastal zone is typically Mediterranean, with olive groves and cultivated fields. Much of the flora is common to southern Spain and Italy.

The montane flora of the Atlas is centred around the cedar forests. These were once far more prolific. In the Middle Atlas of Morocco they form an especially beautiful habitat. Fragments of this forest extend as far as eastern Algeria. Even in summer, wild-

Acacia thorns

life can still be discovered amongst the cedars, while snow is not uncommon during the winter months.

The third zone is the Sahel, which fringes the desert. It is typified by a tussock grass. The Sahel vegetation to the south of the desert, where it borders with Mali and Nigeria, is called cram-cram. Here the grass is interspersed with small acacia trees.

We will mention a few species here, as they extend across the three countries considered in this book and often form the dominant vegetation.

The date palm (*Phoenix dactylifera*) is of great importance because of its crop, harvested each autumn. After the dates have been collected, the palm fronds are cut back, leaving the stumps which form the characteristic edge of the tree. Palms can draw moisture from the water table below and can tolerate partial covering by sand. Nonetheless, date farmers near Tozeur (Tunisia) and Tarhit (Algeria) wage a constant battle against the sea of sand that is for ever blowing across the palmeries. Many of these palmeries — forests of palms — have a population in excess of a quarter of a million trees.

The diverse trees and shrubs of the Acacia family are common throughout the region. Commonly known as wattle trees they originated in Australia. They were introduced to north Africa because of their beauty, and the value of their wood. A number of species grow along the coast and have spread southwards, naturalising in the Sahel regions. They produce fluffy, yellow, pea-sized flowers. The blue-leaved wattle has been used extensively in parts of the Atlas for stabilising the soil. The yellow flowers are large and the leaves are long and lanceolate. In the desert, acacia are important for sustaining plant communities. Their root nodules are packed with bacteria that can convert nitrogen into nitrates. This helps the plants survive in an otherwise mineral-deficient soil.

Eucalyptus is widespread along the Mediterranean coast, but has naturalised to form large woodland areas. The most abundant species is probably the blue gum tree, of which there are extensive areas at Kenitra, north of Rabat, and around Tozeur in Tunisia. It was introduced in the belief that it would help reduce the population of malarial mosquitoes.

The growth of esparto grass has produced a steppeland on the edge of the desert. The competition for nutrients means that little else can grow. Even the esparto fights its neighbours by chemical warfare. Poisons are secreted from its roots to discourage other root systems from encroaching. There is thus a clearly defined boundary around each plant within which nothing else can grow.

Tamarisk is a bush with very narrow branches and leaves that have been reduced to tiny scales. Its long root systems can obtain water from a very great depth, while its tolerance of salt allows it to grow in conditions where other bushes could never survive. It lives in dried-up river beds, often in close proximity to the beautiful oleander bush. This pink-flowered bush has long, grey, leathery leaves. The oleander can form very dense patches of vegetation in an otherwise desolate area.

Crossing an arid plain, it can be a pleasant surprise to find an area of low growing plants, which are obviously melons. This desert melon should be avoided. Many animals can tolerate the succulent fruit, but they induce vomiting in humans.

Plants which are adapted to deserts and can tolerate drought conditions are known as xerophytes. Various adaptations enable them to survive:

1. annual plants have a rapid life-cycle, which ends in the rainy season (e.g. grasses), or they have deep tap roots to reach water (e.g. acacia)
2. reduced leaf area, with spines, hairs or scales to slow water loss
3. succulent leaves and stems to store water
4. in dry conditions leaves drop, together with any salt that has built up
5. spines and thorns prevent grazing animals from removing leaves
6. dual root systems: surface roots to collect quickly any rain and deep roots to reach the water table
7. the ability to absorb water from dry soil
8. different metabolic systems (e.g. photosynthesis).

Aridity is not the only problem that organisms have to face. Saline soil is common as evaporation brings salt to the surface. The degree of salinity varies enormously but it is characterised by a specially adapted vegetation – the halophytes. Many of the species found here have relatives in Europe living on saltmarshes, e.g. glasswort. This has no leaves, but a succulent green stem. Many halophytes have glands for excreting the salt from the plant.

Under the flat stones of the hamada, lichens and microscopic algae grow. Most are adapted to shady conditions. There is just enough light for them beneath the pebbles. Water is obtained from the condensation that occasionally occurs at night.

A hummingbird hawk moth visiting bramble flowers, Middle Atlas

Fauna

A varied range of animals live in north Africa, but it is inevitably the poisonous varieties that achieve notoriety. Extreme environmental conditions necessitate extreme adaptations. Hence, the desert areas support a number of potentially dangerous animals.

Insects

Butterflies abound on the coastal fringes during spring and early summer. Up in the mountains their flying phase extends well into the summer months if nectar is still available. Brambles attract many species, including an array of fritillaries and hummingbird hawk moths. Grasshoppers, crickets and locusts are all common, but it is only when they appear in huge numbers that they become a serious pest. *Eugaster spinulosus* is a very impressive grasshopper with a body length of over 5 cm. It is black and red (often with areas of orange and yellow) with short spines projecting from its thorax. These slow crawling insects are wingless. They are widespread between the mountains and the edge of the desert, and are often to be seen on walls. The colours act as a warning to potential

A darkling beetle, one of the commonest insects of north Africa

predators. If disturbed they give off an evil-smelling liquid from their legs.

Preying mantis are common in bushes to the north. A brown species, *Eremiaphila*, is abundant on the stony desert. It runs quickly, and is perfectly camouflaged when still. They are frequently seen in the High Atlas, around Todra.

Beetles are one of the groups of insects that are best adapted to desert conditions. Most species stay underground during the day and emerge at night. That is the best time to hunt for animals. Darkling beetles are the most abundant. They are part of a large family group called tenebrionids. None of the desert species has wings. Instead, there is an air space beneath their wing cases, which provides insulation against the heat. It also helps to trap moisture.

Beetles are scavengers. *Anthia venator,* is a common carnivorous beetle with white spots on the wing cases. These spots have been shown to reduce the insect's body temperature considerably. Food is scarce for all these species, so some are able to survive for many years without it.

Looking across a dune landscape, it may seem to be totally devoid of life. In the early morning, however, there are signs everywhere of animal movements during the night. Beetle tracks criss-cross the sand. Following the tracks of a jerboa, you may well come across disturbed sand that indicates a struggle, and the remains of a beetle's exoskeleton.

Arachnids

Arachnids are superbly adapted to arid conditions, with a thick, waxy cuticle to prevent waterloss. Three main subgroups are found in north Africa: scorpions, spiders and camel spiders. Scorpions are nocturnal. By day they live curled up in a covered depression, under a rock or boulder, for example. Be careful, as exposed sleeping bags and shoes are tempting habitats. Scorpions are unlikely to sting unless provoked. They are carnivorous and cannibalistic, deriving most of the moisture they need from their prey. Having attempted to sting their prey they are unlikely to chase it. Their eyesight is poor, but they can feel vibrations on the ground through a pair of 'combs' called pectines, which are underneath the body. There are half a dozen or more species common in north Africa. The dark brown *Androctonus australis*, with its large, broad tail, is probably the most venomous of all scorpions. Its sting attacks the nervous system, resulting in death within five hours. This species is found in Tunisia and Algeria.

Camel-spiders (or wind-scorpions) are a unique group. They have no sting, but possess the largest jaws of any animal relative to its size. These nocturnal creatures are so quick and powerful that scorpions are their main prey. The specimens most frequently seen in north Africa (*Galeodes granti*) are just a few centimetres in length, with a bulbous head and sensory organs in their front legs. At an early stage in their life-cycle, specimens less than a centimetre long can be seen catching flies in the early evening. To find them, you will have to lift a rock, while someone else keeps an eye on where they run to.

Spiders are not often seen in the Sahara, although a number of interesting species can be found in the Atlas. These include certain types of tarantula, although these varieties never reach the proportions usually associated with this name. *Argiope lobata* is an orb-web spider, abundant in oases and dry scrub areas. Its white, crinkled abdomen provides camouflage by acting as a disruptive pattern against the pale background.

Amphibians and reptiles

The Sahara is perhaps the last place in which one would think of looking for amphibians. Those that do live there are remnants of the fauna that inhabited this area when it was fertile. They live in the oases, staging a tremendous chorus during the night and early morning. One of the most impressive oasis inhabitants is the very large, yellow and brown-spotted Mauritanian toad (*Bufo mauritanicus*) (see p.72). Leaving the damp areas, it shelters in palmeries by day, hunting at night. It sits for long periods of time, oblivious to human interruption, waiting for its prey – insects, spiders and occasionally small rodents. Most of the noise in the oases comes from the green frog (*Rana ridibunda perezi*). This is a subspecies of the green frog. It is usually seen sitting in the water, croaking.

North Africa supports a wide range of reptiles, including skinks, vipers and tortoises (near the coast). Skinks are fascinating. They live in the ergs and appear to 'swim' through it, hence their common name of sand fish. Yellowish-brown in colour, they have very tight-fitting jaws so that sand cannot pass into their mouths when buried. Their meat is highly prized, and even gets a mention in the Bible.

More than a dozen species of lizard live in north Africa. One of the most interesting is the spiny-tailed lizard (*Uromastyx acanthinurus*), common from southern Morocco to Tunisia. The largest specimens are up to 40 cm in length. As well as living in the desert they also inhabit the semi-desert areas that fringe the Atlas. Colouring varies from green, through yellow and orange, to red. Spiny-tailed lizards are omnivorous, feeding on insects, fruit and young shoots. They eat early in the morning, and then bask in the sun until midday. After spending the afternoon in a burrow, they finish feeding and return to the burrow for the night. Further north, the larger specimens are hunted by man for food, or to sell to passing tourists.

The desert monitor (*Varanus griseus*) is more than a metre in length and eats lizards and small birds. It feeds by day and lives in dry river valleys (although it is fairly abundant in parts of the Hoggar).

Perhaps the most unpleasant reptile you may chance to encounter is the horned viper. This highly poisonous snake averages 50 cm in length. The viper buries itself in the sand, with the form of its body just visible below the surface. During the day, it often buries itself beneath tamarisk bushes, with only its two horns protruding above the sand. It feeds on lizards and jerboas.

Birds

You will find it very useful to take a bird identification book to any of the countries we discuss. Most European bird studies are suitable for the north coast, while the *Collins Guide to Birds of West Africa* is helpful south of the Atlas. Desert oases sound tropical with the warbling of bulbuls and babblers. These are the areas in which you are the most likely to encounter bird life, because of the abundance of food. On the stony desert or in dry river valleys, you may well disturb small flocks of sand grouse. Out on the rocky plains the black and white shape of the white-rumped black chat is a familiar sight. Black is a common colour for natural desert camouflage. Vultures and kites are common in mountainous areas.

The white-rumped black chat or wheatear

Mammals

The most impressive animals of the Middle Atlas are undoubtedly the Barbary apes. Paradoxically, they are not apes at all, but a type of macaque. They form small troupes in the Cedar forests. It takes considerable luck and good eyesight to spot them as they are very shy and quickly disappear to the tops of the trees.

The most frequently encountered desert species is the jerboa. Commonly known as 'kangaroo rats', they come out at night and feed on almost anything. Insects and seeds are favoured foodstuffs, as both of these enable the animals to produce metabolic water. This allows them to survive without drinking. If you are camping in the desert they sometimes approach your tent at night in small groups.

One of the jerboa's predators is the fennec, a pale sandy-coloured fox. It has very large ears, which improves its directional hearing for prey capture. In addition, the large skin area helps in body cooling. The fennec can survive for several days without drinking, but it still has to make regular visits to an oasis or water hole. Fennecs occasionally eat scorpions, in which case they adroitly bite off the sting first.

Gazelles are the only large herbivore to be found in this region. They graze on thorn bushes and dried grass. Often their small herds will be seen in terrain that appears devoid of vegetation.

When you consider popular perceptions of the perfect desert animal, the dromedary camel reigns supreme. Their adaptations are numerous: their huge, flat feet float over the sand without sinking; their nostrils are closable slits; long, thick eyelashes prevent sand from blowing into their eyes; special blood vessels at the base of the brain prevent it from overheating; the ability to metabolise fat to produce water, coupled with their fatty hump means that they can go without drinking for long periods (although this seriously depletes the fat store and makes them look in bad condition), and finally, reduced kidney activity prevents excessive water loss.

It is impossible to describe all the species you might come across here. We offer suggestions for further reading in 'Sources of Information', p.36.

When travelling through north Africa you will often be approached by local people, offering to sell you animals. Lizards, terrapins, ground squirrels and even cuddly fennec fox cubs (watch out for rabies) may be offered for sale. Selling many of these animals, especially the fennecs, is illegal. Even buying them in order to release them serves little purpose as they will soon be recaught. It is best to leave well alone. If all travellers do this then, hopefully, the practice will disappear.

Fossils and minerals

North African rocks are mainly derived from marine sediments. Even so, it is still a surprise to come across the fossils of sea creatures ten thousand feet up in the High Atlas. Although it is comparatively easy to find specimens yourself in the mountains, many exciting fossils and minerals will be thrust under your nose by local children. Trilobites, ammonites and belemnites are particularly popular. The first of these are especially common. You can obtain a 3 or 4 cm specimen for a few pence. Phacops is one of the largest trilobites known. These jet-black specimens carry a high price, so you will have to barter well. The small roadside shacks from where fossils and minerals are sold are fascinating. Many of the fossils are cut and polished. Belemnites are a form of mollusc that the Africans call 'fish'. These abundant fossils are sectioned and polished before they are sold.

Some of the minerals are spectacular. Morocco is famous for its amethyst, while southern Tunisia is liberally scattered with desert

Phacops – a fossil trilobite from the Atlas mountains

rose. Do not be fooled by the astonishing coloured minerals that children hawk in Morocco – it is amazing what you can do with quartz crystals and red and blue dye.

The Peoples of North Africa

There is a wide diversity of cultures and ethnic groups in north Africa. The coastal fringe is primarily populated by an Arab race. Darker skin colours in Tunisia arise from the Negro Sudanese who were once enslaved here. The Arabs are the extroverts of north Africa – hard bargainers and talented linguists (most speak some English, French and German). In the hills and mountains, the Berbers are retiring by comparison. They keep themselves to themselves, and often speak only their own language. Shyly agreeing to be photographed, their children have beautiful faces. Many Berbers are nomadic, living in large black tents made from a heavy woven wool. The Tuaregs are a proud, tall race. Some are still nomadic, although they have many permanent villages in the south of Algeria. Many of the small cafés on the edge of the desert are run by Tuaregs.

A desert market in southern Morocco. In these areas the mixture of races is especially marked, with Berbers, Arabs, Tuaregs and black Africans

The hospitality of all these races is unsurpassed. In material terms, they may have little to offer, but you will still often be asked into their homes. These are opportunities not to be missed. On most occasions you will be offered delicious mint tea: made with boiling water, fresh mint and lots of sugar, cut from a block. The tea is stewed for a long time in an ornate teapot. This may be accompanied by peeled prickly pears or couscous. Even if the food seems less than appetising, you should at least try it, for politeness's sake. You will usually be introduced to the entire family.

The Islamic religion, though suffering from the same spread of secularisation that has affected Christianity in Europe, is a dominant force in north African life. In Morocco, non-Moslems are not allowed to enter mosques. In Tunisia, you are allowed everywhere but the prayer-hall. You must be decently dressed, although the larger mosques will lend you a djellabah, if you have too much skin on show. Show respect if you take any photographs in a mosque. The faithful are called to prayer five times each day, by a 'muezzin' (or a recording of one) from the top of a minaret. The first call of the day is (unfortunately) as early as 4 am. The last finishes by 11 at night.

PLANNING AND PREPARATION

The Land Rover remains the ultimate 4x4 for north African exploration. Here a 12-year-old ex-military Safari demonstates its capability at the Overlander Training Centre in Devon

Introduction

With any independently organised journey to north Africa, it is essential to begin planning and preparing well in advance. School or youth group leaders will need a rough itinerary and costing as much as twelve months in advance, in order to give the participants time to find the money. Similarly, you will need a rough plan early on if you are approaching companies and other organisations for financial or material support.

'Mental Preparations'

Culture shock

From the moment that you land in Africa, the sudden change in culture and lifestyle is obvious. If Algeciras and the countryside of southern Spain seemed 'uncivilised', then Morocco will appear to be a whole new world. Beggars and trinket-sellers hassle you on the street, while small children crowd round, demanding *un stylo* or *une cigarette*. It is very easy to become detached and aloof, regarding the people as though they were attractions in a safari park.

Galeodes – the wind scorpion or camel spider

'Culture shock' is not just a vogue phrase. For those who have never left the relative affluence of Western Europe, seeing the different ways in which people live their lives elsewhere can be quite disturbing.

Especially in Algeria and Morocco, both rural and urban poverty can be quite severe. This has an obvious effect on the health of the people. In desert regions, a lack of variation in diet can cause problems through vitamin deficiency. Tuareg nomads have often asked us to tend open sores, while in the Atlas it is not uncommon for people to appear complaining of headaches and asking for drugs. This is often the only way in which medicine can be obtained, so the chances are that the headache is probably fictitious.

After camping rough in the open countryside, you should always bury any rubbish that is to be left behind. This conscientious act, however, may soon be undone. As you leave, dozens of children often rush in and dig the rubbish up, searching for mineral-water bottles and other useful items.

Having warned you of the impact of 'culture shock' it is important to emphasise that one can never really come to know north Africa by simply passing through, as though hermetically sealed from the outside world. North Africans are wonderfully friendly, and they are rightfully proud of their hospitality. You are unlikely to spend more than a week in any one of the countries that we describe without being invited to someone's house. Although some judgement is obviously necessary, you would be foolish to decline all such invitations. Even when there is practically no shared language, these situations provide a marvellous opportunity to see how different peoples live.

Guides

Generally speaking, guides are rarely essential in north Africa, but there are places in which they can be useful. Often a 'guided tour' can give a good overall impression of a city, leaving you to return alone to the areas which you find most interesting. This is undoubtedly the case in Fes, but not in Algiers or Tunis. Consequently, we have suggested in the main text where guides would be useful. Guides are not only useful in urban areas. For example, they are a great help in finding rock paintings in rural Algeria.

In places where you want to find a guide, the chances are that they will find you first. Indeed, more often than not you will be spoilt for choice. Many of the guides that take the initiative in approaching

Street sellers in Marrakech, bargaining with a European family

you are unlicensed. Confirmation will be provided if they temporarily disappear when the police come into view. Nonetheless, they are often as good as official guides, and usually cheaper. Having said this, if you are looking for something in particular, it is probably sensible to ask the hotel or campsite manager to recommend someone (although it will probably be his brother-in-law!).

A brief warning: in Morocco it is not unknown for an unofficial guide to take you into the centre of the souks and then demand money to get you out. If you refuse point blank to pay, you can always give a passing child a few coins to get you out. It is essential, though, to know the name of the place that you want to be led back to. A good guide will tell you where to aim for if the group becomes separated.

Vehicles and Transport in North Africa

Tunisia, Algeria and Morocco together encompass an area of more than 3 million sq.km – some twelve times the size of the United Kingdom. Although some form of local transport is nearly always available, independent travel is advisable if you hope to cover large

Public transport may be rather basic. Here in the High Atlas, Morocco, the lorry contains cattle below with the passengers on top

distances in a relatively short period of time. Even in Tunisia, where the bus services are both frequent and extensive, it is surprising how much difference having one's own vehicle makes to the time required to complete a circuit of the country. In rural and mountainous areas of Morocco, an informal public transport system operates, based on the rugged trucks that are used to carry livestock and agricultural produce to market. Trains can be useful for covering long distances between major centres, but buses are far more flexible.

Car hire is straightforward but very expensive. For example, you will have to allow £300 sterling per week in Tunisia. There are no dominant local car-hire firms – Avis and Hertz control the market. With offices at the international airports, these companies can arrange to have your car waiting for you on arrival. Hire cars only come with third-party insurance. Comprehensive cover is very expensive.

What vehicle to take

If you decide to travel with your own vehicle, consider your requirements carefully before deciding what to take. Any family car will do if you intend to stick with tarmac roads. It is worth remembering that French models dominate the market in north Africa, so these present fewest problems if you need to find spares. With other cars, this can prove difficult. Fortunately, though, Arab mechanics tend to be very adaptable and can 'modify' most spares to fit!

Driving off-road, a Land Rover or some other four-wheel drive vehicle comes into its own. Having said this, one should never be surprised to see a Renault 4 or a 2CV emerge from the most inhospitable conditions. Their lightness makes them flexible, while low fuel consumption is another considerable advantage. On the downside, they are lacking in the amount they can carry. This can be crucial for especially long journeys. For example, desert crossings such as the Tanezrouft, in Algeria, involve carrying enough fuel and water for 1,500 km. Four-wheel drive vehicles are indispensable for routes involving much sand or hill-climbing.

For many years the Land Rover has been the favourite vehicle for desert travellers. You will encounter this vehicle throughout north Africa. This means that spares, new and old, are not a major problem, and many mechanics are experienced at working with them. They are reliable and can carry considerable loads.

In the early 1980s Land Rover brought out a new series of vehicles. These were the 110 in and 90 in wheel-bases, with permanent four-wheel drive (the former carries less, but is better for rough terrain, as the middle does not 'bottom out'). Possible engine types include a V8 and 2.5 litre petrol and turbo diesel versions. These are very different from earlier Land Rovers both in terms of comfort and engineering. The replacement of leaf springs by coil springs has made the ride smoother, but partly reduced the amount of 'overloading' possible. The ability of the new 90 to pull itself through mud, however, is astounding. Over recent years, the Toyota Land Cruiser and the Nissan Patrol have begun to threaten Land Rover's dominance.

For a major expedition into the desert, it is vital to make the right choice of vehicle, and to prepare carefully. The *Sahara Handbook* discusses these problems in greater depth.

Documentation

You will need a Green Card, a GB sticker on the rear of the vehicle and an International Driving Licence (available from the AA or RAC). A Carnet du Passage is necessary for some countries (see the relevant chapters) or if you intend to travel between countries. AA Five Star Insurance covers north Africa.

Off-road Driving Techniques

A surprising proportion of the north African road network has been asphalted. Unfortunately, on routes such as the road to Tamanrasset the number of potholes makes the surface worse than the original gravel plain. Hitting these at speed can damage both tyres and steering.

A common road surface to encounter is 'piste' – desert track, sometimes improved by scraping. This process invariably produces a corrugated surface, especially when used by heavy traffic. The small, regular ridges are best taken at speed to reduce vehicle shake. (In some places, though, the corrugations can be as much as 50 cm wide, when driving at speed is both difficult and dangerous.) Nuts and bolts should be checked at the end of each journey – and do not expect the doors to fit as well as once they did!

Driving on hamada (rocky desert) is straightforward enough. Four-wheel drive need only be engaged when the going gets rough. The problems come when crossing sand. It is easy to become bogged down in soft, deep sand ('feche feche'). Use low range in soft sand, to provide enough power to push through, but not enough to spin the wheels. Choice of gear depends on engine power, e.g. 3rd with a Range Rover, 2nd with a 2.25 litre petrol-driven Land Rover. Try to avoid changing gear as the drag of the sand may slow you down too much as you do so. If the vehicle halts and the wheels begin to spin, stop immediately, before you become totally bogged down. Facing drifts of sand blown across a tarmac road, it is tempting to use speed to get through it. Beware, though, you are more likely to put the vehicle out of control and damage the suspension.

If you are likely to encounter soft sand, it is worth using sand tyres. These are balloon-like with a minimum of tread. Traction on any tyre can be increased by reducing the pressure by 50–75 per cent (although this makes a remarkable difference to the traction as you float across the sand). Make sure the pressure is restored to normal when you reach stony ground. If you are likely to use this technique frequently, a carbon dioxide cylinder is much less bother than a foot pump. Remember that driving in heat will increase the tyre pressure automatically. A midday drive on tarmac can double it. This problem is reduced by inflating tyres with carbon dioxide or nitrogen, although this is little help if you need to deflate and reinflate in the middle of the desert.

In difficult conditions it is best to drive in convoy. If the first vehicle gets stuck there is always one behind to help pull it out.

Winches on the front of a vehicle are very expensive and invariably require a land anchor if another vehicle is not available. Even then a well-bogged Land Rover could be difficult to winch out if attached to another one. An effective, cheaper alternative is a high-lift jack. The end of the vehicle can be jacked up by over a metre and then pushed to one side, clear of the ruts in which it was stuck. In this way it can be manoeuvred sideways. When unbogging a vehicle it may be easiest to lift the wheels on to sand ladders. These are aluminium sheets or girders which allow you to gather enough speed to keep going. This means that you may not be able to stop until you see harder ground, so the rest of the 'crew' will have to walk behind.

Ditches should always be tackled at an angle, to prevent 'bottoming out'. If you have to drive along a V-shaped gully, someone should walk backwards in front of the vehicle, to ensure that the wheels remain at the same level, so there is no danger of rolling over.

All these techniques require practice, so it is well worth attending an off-road driving course. This will give you greater confidence in your vehicle's potential. Details (and a wide range of books) are available from David Bowyer, Overlander, Off Road Centre, East Foldhay, Zeal Monachorum, Crediton, Devon, EX17 6DH. Land Rover produce a free booklet on driving techniques, available from their Consumer Services Department in Solihull.

Camping and Accommodation

In many ways, north Africa is ideal for camping. Rain is rare and the evenings so equable that you hardly need a tent. A dining shelter is sufficient as it gives shade during the day and a well-ventilated roof at night. Other than agricultural land, there are few restrictions on camping. Take plenty of spare pegs if you camp during the summer. The ground is either like rock, when you need a drill to get the pegs into the earth or it is loose sand, and the pegs refuse to stay in place. Rocks can be used instead of, or in addition to, pegs when ground conditions are difficult.

In a hot atmosphere, tents can be unbearable. Manufacturers such as Trigano give their fly-sheets a heat-reflective silvered finish. You can improvise by fixing a thin foil emergency blanket over your fly-sheet.

There are many ways to provide lighting for tents. The best idea is to use a fluorescent tube light powered by a vehicle battery.

These last for hours without running the battery down. Coleman also produce petrol-powered lights.

Your choice of sleeping bag is only important if you intend to be in the desert during winter, when the temperature can drop to freezing. It is a good idea to take cotton inner linings for sleeping bags. These can be washed regularly, and can be used on their own on hot nights. You can make your own from a doubled-over cotton sheet.

Security is always a problem when camping. Stay in an official site if you are near a large settlement. These municipal campsites are usually located near the newer city areas and have high walls or fences. At night they have armed guards, to keep thieves at bay. If possible, set your tent near the centre of the camp, away from the perimeter. The number of fellow campers (and the state of the swimming pool) will depend on the time of the year. Near the Sahara, spring and autumn are the high season.

The risk of theft diminishes as you move away from the towns and the Mediterranean coast. Even so, a number of basic precautions are advisable wherever you camp. Do not leave anything outside your tent or vehicle. Always place bags and valuables in the middle of the tent, as thieves sometimes slit the bottom at night, reach inside and remove bags laid along the edges. Placing plastic bin liners in the edges of the tent is a deterrent, as they rustle if someone puts their hand in. Always keep your passport and money inside your sleeping bag with you. Most of these problems are associated with populous areas. There is certainly no need to become paranoid.

The quality of hotels varies widely. In isolated areas you may have a room with a bed, or, for less money, a communal area where you are given rugs and large cushions. The bottom line in accommodation is to sleep on the roof. This is perfect for the desert. Generally speaking, charges only cover accommodation, and not food. If you are a teacher leading a group, point this out to the proprietor, who may give you preferential rates.

Staying in a small, cheap hotel is an ideal way to meet the locals, who will be a useful source of information on routes and accommodation. You will often be asked to share their food and drink.

Food and Drink

In contrast to Morocco and Tunisia, *fresh fruit and vegetables* can be scarce and expensive in Algeria.You can barter for these in the markets, which also sell meat and fish. Unfortunately, *meat and other protein sources* tend to be of dubious quality. If you have to eat locally bought meat, cut it into small chunks and fry or boil them thoroughly. *Eggs* are a good source of protein that is both cheap and relatively sterile.

Given these problems, we would suggest taking *dehydrated meat or soya meals*. A number of UK manufacturers produce these, including McDougalls of Reading who make an excellent range of complete meals. They are available from your local Cash and Carry, in resealable tubs that can be made up to 5 lb or 12 lb weight. The chicken curry is particularly good. You need not eat these all the time, but they are a good insurance. McDougalls also make excellent dehydrated fruit juices, called Refresh. The crystals, which come in sealed packets, can be added to bottles of mineral water. Even if you are flying out it is easy enough to carry some of these products. The question of whether you should take your own food from the UK is academic for the backpacker. For the larger group, though, it is an important problem. Sources of food are scarce in isolated areas. If you do find one, they may be unwilling to disappoint regular customers by exhausting their stocks for tourists. Even if you intend to buy all your food locally, it is worth taking a small reserve supply.

Camping Gaz is the most popular cooking fuel for independent travellers. Supplies, though, can be scarce and expensive. The tanks are bulky and the flame almost useless in windy conditions.

Cooking with petrol is quicker and much cheaper in the long run. Optimus burners are ideal for the lone backpacker or small group. Coleman burners can cope with up to three pans at a time. The petrol is forced as vapour from a hand-pumped pressurised chamber. Cooking technique is thus the same as with gas. If leaded petrol is used, the burners will have to be cleaned regularly. You should take a supply of spare pumps and generators.

Bread is plentiful in all north African countries. You will have to ask a local to show you where the bakeries are, as they rarely have signs. In some towns the bakery simply deals with dough brought in by families, and does not sell to passers-by. Little children can frequently be seen running through the streets carrying loaves on their heads. Bread in the markets tends to be well handled, which can be off-putting. The Arabs have a sweet tooth, so sticky cakes are common.

Cooked food from the souks can be filling and cheap. Often you pay a fixed price and then help yourself to a selection of fried or barbecued food. Obviously, you have to make your own judgment as to the 'safety' of what's on offer. Roast chicken is common, as is 'couscous' – steamed semolina with vegetables and meat. Omelette and chips is always a good safe option.

Mineral water is widely available in 1.5 litre bottles. This is far more pleasant than tablet-purified water, unless you buy Ain Okta in Tunisia, which tastes like a mouthful of the average British municipal swimming pool. Many locals drink Coke and Fanta, as their decayed teeth suggest. North African beers are generally tasteless chemical brews.

In the desert you may need to take *water from a well*. Water sometimes lies hundreds of metres below the surface, in huge subterranean lakes confined by non-porous rock. Wells are easily recognisable by their surrounding walls (and pillars if the well is deep). Wooden covers are put on top when the well is not in use.

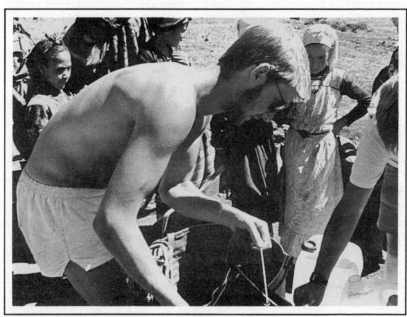

Telouet, High Atlas: collecting water from a village well

Buckets are not always kept on the spot, so you may have to borrow one from a local. They are usually made of leather, so that they collapse and sink below the water, filling as they are pulled up. Standard plastic buckets are of little use, as they float on the surface of the water.

Health

Although the Marrakech Two-Step and the Tangier Trots are legendary problems for the traveller, they are not unavoidable, given some planning and foresight.

Inoculations and Disease

Make sure your tetanus jabs are up-to-date. Views on what other injections are necessary tend to differ, so consult your GP before travelling. It is worth having the cholera/typhoid jab and topping up your polio. Gamma globulin injections give considerable protection from hepatitis, which can result from poor sanitation. Malaria is much less a problem in north than central Africa, but it is worth taking the prophylactic drugs obtainable from your chemist. All these precautions need planning well before departure. The cholera/typhoid jab can have unpleasant side effects, so arrange it well in advance. You should be aware that some inoculations have a limited period of effectiveness – gamma globulin lasts for only six months.

Bilharzia is a parasite, whose secondary host is the water snail. Stagnant or slow-moving water, with plenty of green weed, is the ideal habitat for these snails, although the parasite may not be present. It is best to avoid swimming or standing in water of this type. The danger is greater the further south you go. Clear water without weed is generally safe. Bilharzia is a debilitating, rather than a fatal disease. The most obvious symptom is blood in the urine. It can be treated.

Diarrhoea

Few people manage to survive for long in north Africa without suffering from diarrhoea at some time. It can be avoided to some extent by carefully washing food, purifying drinking water and avoiding too much sun. Diarrhoea can be treated with Immodium or Lomotil, but you should consult a doctor if symptoms persist. It is important for sufferers to maintain their fluid and mineral levels. Fluids should be taken regularly, with Rehydrate, Dioralyte or an equivalent powder dissolved in them. Electrosol also helps re-store mineral balance, and is available in tablet form from chemists.

Heat Exhaustion

To avoid heat exhaustion, wear a hat and remain covered up until you gradually acclimatise to the conditions. Arriving in the desert from the chilly UK puts considerable strain on the body. It must have time to rest and adjust to the heat. Initially, you will sweat and lose too much salt – the cause of heat exhaustion. Especially in the first week, you should add extra salt to your food, or take salt pills, e.g. Electrosol. The first symptoms are tiredness and cramp, followed by nausea. Sufferers must stay in the shade and rest.

Animal Bites and Stings

Dog bites in Africa carry a danger of rabies. If you suspect that the dog might have the disease you must go to a major city for treatment. Vaccines are not always available, in which case you may decide to return home immediately for treatment.

A scorpion at rest

North Africa is home to several deadly scorpions, although the majority of stings are simply painful. There are few treatments except ice (if you can get it) or an injection of anti-venom, which must be stored at low temperatures. The anti-venom can be obtained before you leave the UK. You are unlikely to see scorpions without turning over rocks and boulders. Even then they rarely attack, but remain still in their small hollows. Rocks should always be lifted with the opening away from you, in case camel spiders lurk beneath. These are not deadly, but have a powerful bite.

The deadly horned viper lives just under the surface of sand, especially beneath tamarisk bushes. Their side-winder tracks can be seen on the sand.

Food and Water

With plentiful supplies available, it is tempting to gorge yourself on fruit, inevitably leading to diarrhoea. Wash all fruit with either heavily chlorinated water or a solution of potassium permanganate. Puritabs and Steritabs are branded chemicals for chlorinating water. The active ingredient is potassium isocyanurate, which can be ordered through a chemist. As only a tiny quantity is needed, this is cheaper and less bulky than the tablets. Alternatively, boiling water for ten minutes will kill any pathogens. Locally butchered meat should be washed well, to remove flies' eggs as well as bacteria. (See 'Food and Drink', p.27, above).

Avoid local ice creams and ice in drinks and salads, because of the risk of contaminated water.

Washing

Toilets are primitive at best and washing facilities are generally poor. If you have your own vehicle, a useful item is a resealable container half filled with Savlon or another disinfectant. With a supply of paper towels, this is a hygienic way of washing hands. Concentrated Savlon is available in small sachets. It must be changed once a day.

Showers are normally cold, unless you are staying in an international hotel. Independent travellers could take a garden spray (e.g. Killaspray). These make an ideal portable shower. They are very economical with water – one gallon will give four or five showers.

A large group will generate a considerable quantity of washing up. It can be very difficult to keep a large eating/cooking area hygienic when rough camping. Use a big bucket of sodium isocyanurate solution to store cutlery and crockery between meals. This is the same principle as Milton sterilisation, but far cheaper.

General

A list of common ailments and suggested treatments is given in the checklist at the end of this section. If you are taking a sizeable group abroad, it is well worth cultivating the help of your local GP. S/he will usually be eager to help you with advice or prescriptions.

Clothing

You will have to endure extremes of temperature in north Africa, so several sets of clothing are necessary. In the Algerian Hoggar, in the middle of the Sahara, the wind can make a jacket or pullover essential. Obviously, though, the main problem is the heat. Go for cotton rather than synthetic fibres, and garments that are loose and cover the body. Following local style, you could buy yourself a kaftan or djellabah. A sun-hat is essential.

Even a habitual 'shorts and T-shirt' wearer should keep one set of smarter clothes – useful when dealing with police, customs or other officials. If you have long hair, be prepared to be treated with little respect.

Money and Credit Cards

North African monies cannot be obtained legally outside the countries concerned. At ports such as Algeciras, you may be offered currency by unofficial dealers who claim that there is a bank holiday or strike in your country of destination. Ignore them, as their rates are generally very bad, or at most, change enough money to last for a day. Sterling, francs and dollars may be accepted at some large establishments.

Credit cards are hardly worth taking, except to pay for an emergency air flight if necessary. Travellers cheques are the best way of carrying money. Eurocheques are more widely accepted in Morocco and Tunisia than they are in most of Europe.

All three countries have state-run craft shops which sell carpets, rugs, etc, at fixed prices. There is usually one in each large town. Away from these stores you will be expected to bargain. Bargaining for purchases is the normal procedure. It is very difficult to provide guidelines for bargaining. The secret is to have a clear idea of what an item is really worth to you, and then to offer a price some way lower so that you can haggle upwards. Never bargain for goods you have no intention of buying, and harden your heart towards imaginative stories of the seller's ten starving children.

In the Atlas mountains numerous individuals will offer you minerals and fossils. Many will accept audio tapes in lieu of money. As Western music is difficult to get hold of, this bartering can provide both buyer and seller with a bargain.

Always carry your money and passport in a money belt, or in a purse around your neck that will tuck inside your clothing.

Maps

The Michelin 153 covers the entire area at a scale of 1 cm to 40 km. (Users are even eligible to join a '153 Club'!) Michelin make more detailed maps, such as the 172 series. Some are no longer available because of sensitivity over the Moroccan/Algerian border. Even the 153 will be confiscated in some parts of Algeria. The Hildebrand's Travel Maps of Morocco and Tunisia are very good, and are available from W.H.Smith. Almost all maps can be obtained from Stanfords Map Centre, 12–14 Long Acre, Covent Garden, London WC1. They can be ordered by telephone and, if in stock, will be posted to you on the same day.

Insurance

Insurance is essential. If you are seriously ill it will be costly and you may want to fly home. If you have anything stolen you will need a police report for your insurance claim. There is almost no chance that they will recover your property, which will probably be sold in the local market. The AA have now extended their 5-Star Cover to Morocco, Tunisia and Algeria.

Photography

North Africa presents an endless succession of photographic opportunities. Avoid the temptation to photograph airports, docks or military establishments and personnel. One of our party took a photo of a stork's nest when our vehicle was at a police road-block. The film was ripped from the camera by the policeman. Be careful when photographing people – some are not keen, while others demand money. You may even be charged for taking a picture of someone's camel! Consequently, a telephoto lens is indispensable for candid shots. In situations with a large number of people, such as a market, you can take shots without attracting attention by keeping the camera at your side. Using a wide-angled lens with automatic exposure, focusing is no longer critical.

On the whole, exposures are easy to determine as sky and foreground tend to be of uniform illumination. Problems come when you photograph white buildings or the bright sand of the ergs. You will need to increase the exposure by several stops. For those with automatic cameras this can be done by changing the film speed. For example, if you are using a speed of ISO 100 (see the film packet) set the dial on the camera at ISO 50 or, if it is very bright, ISO 25. The problem is that in very bright conditions the camera is fooled and over-compensates, producing a dark picture. To be on the safe side, an important subject which involves contrasts of brightness should be photographed several times, using the camera's light reading and then your own.

The use of a polarising lens filter will greatly improve the blueness of the sky and cut down slightly on the brightness of subjects.

Film is very expensive in north Africa – if you manage to find any for sale. Try to bring as much as you can from the UK.

Camera cases may look impressive, but they still let in dust and sand. Bring a supply of resealable polythene bags and put cameras in these. Films will be safe in their plastic tubs, but should be kept as cool as possible. Never leave your camera in the sun. The black surfaces absorb so much heat that they can become too hot to handle.

Take a packet of lens tissues and a blower brush to clean lenses of dust and sand. Using a skylight filter will not only absorb ultraviolet light, but it will also protect the lens. Unlike lenses, filters are cheap to replace if they become scratched.

Do not forget to take spare batteries if your camera uses them.

Make sure that your camera equipment is well insured.

Sexual Harassment

In common with all Islamic societies, the countries of north Africa can present problems for female travellers. Outside the larger and more Westernised cities, women are rarely seen in the open. Salespeople are male, as are café owners and their customers. Keeping bare skin to a minimum is prudent, and travelling in a group with at least one man deters most troublemakers. Similarly, in dealings with officialdom, males will be treated with more respect and urgency.

Male homosexuality is far more open and accepted in north Africa than it is in most parts of Europe. Men travelling alone or in unmixed groups are almost certain to be propositioned fairly frequently.

Customs and Officialdom

As with most Third World countries, the authorities in north Africa are keenly bureaucratic. Documents and papers must be in order for frequent inspections. Official-looking documents often impress the authorities, even if they cannot read them. A headmaster's letter – smothered with round rubber-stamp prints – proving that you are a teacher can do wonders. If you are going for more than just a holiday, it is a great help if you can get an 'Attestation' from the tourist board of your destination country. This asks the authorities to give you all possible assistance. Unfortunately, Tunisia is now reluctant to issue these, as a recent Attestation holder spent his time in the country organising a pornography ring!

Partly for these reasons you should allow plenty of time to negotiate customs, especially if you have a vehicle. Patience in such situations is a necessity, not just a virtue. A bloody-minded customs official will not be overly concerned at keeping you stewing for a couple of days. Tales of bribery securing rapid passage through bureaucracy are common. Unless well versed in such techniques, do not risk it.

Keep your passport with you. This is not just for security, but also for convenience, as it is fairly common for vehicles to be stopped and passports demanded. At official campsites or hotels you will have to fill in a form with personal details. This can get very tedious if you are touring and staying somewhere different every night.

Morocco is very sensitive to people's movements. Watch out for random road blocks, particularly at night. These consist of a flat length of bent cast iron with spikes on it, laid across the road. In the dark, people have been known to drive over them, ruining their tyres. At each stop all passports will be checked and more form filling may take place.

Large quantities of hashish are grown in the Rif area of Morocco (see p.50). This is illegal and possession is punishable with a prison sentence. It is not unusual for someone to sell hash to a European, and then inform the police. As the informer is then rewarded, s/he does very well out of the whole process. Our advice is straightforward – do not get involved with hash in any way, or you may be starring in your own remake of 'Midnight Express'. As you leave the country, check that nothing has been hidden in or under your vehicle. Drugs are occasionally planted in this fashion, and then an accomplice in Spain is instructed to relieve you of them when – and if – you get clear of Spanish customs.

Tour Operators

A number of companies specialise in package tours that go a little beyond the run-of-the-mill 'sun and beach' types. These 'adventure' or 'expedition' trips vary in length and cost, according to the degree of involvement and type of accommodation. Look out for advertisements in geographical or birdwatching magazines, or try your local travel agent. One company which deals with north Africa and the Sahara is:

Duncan Gough, Guerba Expeditions Ltd.,
101 Eden Vale Road, Westbury,
Wiltshire BA13 3QX
Brochure details: Tel: 0800 373334

Guerba use specially modified four-wheel-drive Bedford trucks. Most of their customers are between 18 and 40.

Sources of Information

There are a number of excellent general books we would recommend that you consult before making a trip to Africa.

John Hatt, *The Tropical Traveller* (Pan): this paperback does not deal with any one destination, but discusses preparations and problems common to all hot countries.

Simon and Jan Glen, *Sahara Handbook* (Lascelles): *the* book for anyone contemplating a desert expedition. It covers all the countries of the Sahara, but is of little use to the general traveller in Morocco or Tunisia. It deals mainly with trans-Saharan crossings, although considerable detail is given to routes in Algeria. It also discusses vehicles (in good depth), health problems and history.

Sahara Desert (Pergamon: Key Environment Series): each chapter is written by a specialist. It deals with all aspects of the desert including the fauna and flora, geology, climate and human geography.

General literature can be obtained from each country's tourist office – the addresses are given at the end of the book. The Royal Geographical Society Library (4, Kensington Gore, London) is helpful in providing detailed information about remote locations. You do not have to be a member, although this can be useful if you become really involved in world travel. The RGS also run an Expedition Advisory Centre. The EAC compiles brief details of the expeditions that travel each year in *The Expedition Yearbook*. They also have a large collection of full expedition reports which you can read.

Equipment Checklists

Vehicle spares

Particular reference is given to petrol-driven Land Rovers. Your local vehicle distributor, Unipart dealer or motor accessory shop will be able to modify this list to suit your particular vehicle.

fuel pump repair kit
exhaust valve
decoke set
spark plugs
distributor cap
coil
contact set
condenser
rotor arm
reconditioned water pump
carburettor kit
brake hoses for front and rear
front and rear axle kits
slave cylinder kit

clutch master cylinder kit
bushes and shackle pin
universal joint
brake master cylinder kit
S/H rear half shaft
set of light bulbs
fuel pump
fan belt
set of radiator hoses and heater hoses
radiator cap
hose clips
clutch plate and cover
release bearing
2 litres of brake/clutch fluid
1 litre of gear oil EP90
exhaust bandages and silencer repair paste
instant gasket
3 m length of petrol pipe
rad seal
petrol patches
hose bandage
epoxy resin
WD 40 or equivalent
engine oil – calculate amount and then double it; Land Rovers tend
to be thirsty for oil, especially if the terrain is hard going
2 short-handled shovels
range of spanners, sockets etc.
hammer, screw drivers, hacksaw
insulating tape
emery cloth, assorted nuts & bolts, screws

This is the list of items we would carry for a 5-week trip. You will find that many guide books include a list four times its length. Other things could go wrong but these items have always covered the problems that we have encountered. They will also pack into one large box. You have to strike a balance. The shorter your trip, and the greater the availability of spares in your destination, the fewer items you need to take.

Medical supplies

The following list suggests treatment for the most common ailments found in a group of approximately 18 people staying in remote areas for 4–6 weeks. Contact your GP before you leave, as some useful drugs are only available on prescription.

These are simply suggestions that we have found effective in dealing with the problems that we have come across on our travels. Professional advice must be sought before departure.

Ears, nose and throat

Congestion, catarrh and rhinitis – long-acting decongestant, e.g. Dimotapp

Painful and sore throat – antiseptic painkilling oral rinse, throat lozenges

Intestinal

Diarrhoea and sickness – Immodium for diarrhoea, Lomotil for both. The latter is suitable for children. Persistent diarrhoea causes loss of salts. Rehydrate helps to restore the balance, as do Electrosol tablets.

Vomiting – antiemetic, e.g. Stemitil

Indigestion – antacids

Colic – antispasmodics, e.g. Buscopan (suitable for children)

Travel sickness – e.g. Stugeron

Dressings for cuts, etc.

crêpe bandages
antiseptic swabs
plasters
butterfly sutures
non-allergenic plasters, e.g. Micropore

Other pains and problems

Headache and general pain – painkiller, e.g. paracetamol

Hay fever and other allergies – antihistamine tablets

Chafing and sore skin – an antifungal cream with hydrocortisone and an anti-inflammatory, e.g. Econacort

Insect bites – antihistamine, e.g. Anthisan cream

Muscular pain – e.g. Algesal cream

Eye infection – e.g. Murine eye drops

MOROCCO

Passing a village on the Midelt to Rich road

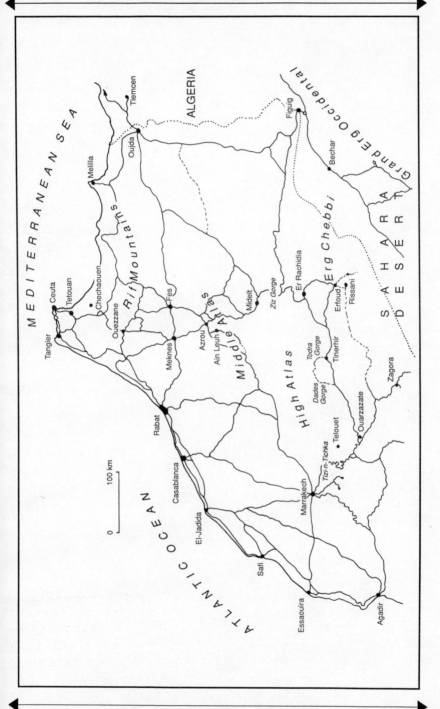

Introduction

Standing at the westernmost limit of the Islamic world, Morocco is a country that captures the emotions like no other. It offers a unique combination of breathtaking scenery, a fascinating culture and the greatest variety of natural habitats in north Africa. Morocco is perhaps the ideal destination for the travelling naturalist who has decided to venture beyond the confines of Europe. It is more accessible than Algeria, while being less westernised than Tunisia. Most of the wildlife to be seen in north Africa will be found somewhere in Morocco.

The kingdom of Morocco is a mountainous nation. Three impressive ranges arc across the landscape. The central range – the Middle Atlas – is fringed with forests rich in wildlife. Further south, the High Atlas mountains have been sliced through by centuries of erosion, to produce spectacular winding gorges. To the south of these, the vast sand oceans of the Sahara stretch away, far into the distance.

Despite the natural attractions that Morocco boasts, no visitor should leave without devoting a few days to the country's wonderful cities. Although the large settlements on the Atlantic coast can prove something of a disappointment, the ancient imperial capitals inland are quite unmissable. Even a short sojourn in Fes or Marrakech will prove to be an unforgettable experience.

Geography

Morocco covers an area of 440,000 km. It is situated in the far north-west of the African continent, bordered by Algeria to the east and Mauritania to the South. As we noted above, Morocco's physical geography is dominated by its mountain ranges. Furthest to the north, the Rif stretch parallel to the Mediterranean coast for 300 km, from Ceuta to Melilla. These limestone mountains, which reach a height of 2,455 m, are forested with olives, oaks and cedars.

Beyond the Fes plain, the Middle Atlas sweep up from south-west to north-east. This range is best known for the extensive cedar forests that cover its slopes. The region is undoubtedly a highlight for the visiting naturalist. South of these mountains there is a wide strip of high, arid plateau leading to the High Atlas. As the name suggests, these mountains are the tallest in Morocco. Jbel Toubkal, at 4,165 m, is the country's highest peak. The best way to appreciate the majesty of this range is to travel through the Todra and Dades gorges. The Dades is not described as the 'Grand Canyon of Morocco' for nothing.

To the south of the High Atlas, you find yourself on the fringe of the Sahara, the world's largest desert. Much of the Moroccan section is stony, scrub speckled plain, rather than the classic dunes of *Beau Geste* and David Lean's *Lawrence of Arabia*. Having said this, there are areas of true erg that remain fairly accessible to the visitor.

Climate

In common with the other countries of north Africa, the best time to visit Morocco is during the Spring. Having said this, most people will be constrained to visit during the summer. In the north, the Mediterranean climate presents no problems at this time of year. Towards the desert, however, the difference can be considerable. With temperatures exceeding 40°C, you will naturally find it difficult to do too much during the middle of the day. If you do not have your own vehicle, this can be a serious handicap. The mountain area, sandwiched between the coastal zone and desert, is relatively cool. As one might imagine, the desert areas are particularly arid. Although there might be as little as 10 cm of rain a year, this tends to come in sudden, destructive downpours.

Driving in Morocco

The quality of Moroccan roads is generally good. Driving in desert areas presents its own special problems. These are dealt with in the 'Planning and Preparation' section, p.24. Care is also required on some of the narrow mountain roads in the High Atlas. These are frequently used by robust trucks. You should be especially cautious when passing them. If the worst comes to the worst, you can gain comfort from the knowledge that Moroccan mechanics are excellent, if a little unorthodox.

Drivers must be at least 21 years of age, and in possession of a Green card and an International Driving Licence.

Maps

The Edition Marcus map of Morocco (1:400,000) is excellent. When buying a map, be careful about the scale. If the disputed Western Sahara territory is included on the same side of the paper as the rest of the country, you may well find that a fair amount of detail is lost.

Currency

The Moroccan dirham is divided into 100 centimes. The dirham is a soft currency, which is to say that it cannot officially be bought outside the country. However, the sharks at the Algeciras ferry terminal are certain to try to tempt you.

Credit cards are of limited use. Only establishments in the largest cities will accept them.

Language

The official language is Arabic, although French is widely spoken. In some parts of the country, Spanish and Berber prevail.

Berber tents in the Middle Atlas

The North-East

The Mediterranean Coast

Ceuta

The position of Ceuta, both politically and geographically, is analagous to that of Gibraltar. Like its northern neighbour, this small enclave seems to cling incongruously to its vast host continent. The peninsula, together with Melilla to the east, is the last remnant of Spanish control over the lands of northern Morocco. (The remainder received its independence in 1956.)

Iberian domination originated in the early fifteenth century. However, Ceuta's historical significance supposedly dates from far earlier. It stands on the promontory of Monte Hacho, which legend decrees to be the southern of the Pillars of Hercules. (Some regard the Jbel Mousa as a more likely candidate, being slightly more similar to the Rock of Gibraltar.)

In Arabic, this 'State Territory' is referred to as Sebta. This linguistic confusion should be borne in mind when consulting some maps, roadsigns and members of Moroccan officialdom. It must be admitted that this Spanish possession contains little of intrinsic interest, with the possible exception of the cathedral of Our Lady of Africa.

Leaving the ferry from Algeciras, there are no customs formalities until you leave Spanish territory. The drive through the blandly prosperous town, and along the coast to the frontier, takes a matter of minutes. Unfortunately, once you join the queue of overheating vehicles, filled with overheating occupants, the time taken to enter Morocco itself lies securely in the lap of Allah. The narrow and filthy road leading to the border is fringed by the Mediterranean on one side, and by a high wall on the other. As the snake of vehicles inches along, heat-resistant Ceutians constantly emerge from the swirling dust to offer water, buns, perfume and ceramics. Their persistent attentions are a mild introduction to the displays of salesmanship to come.

After an eternity of perhaps five hours, you reach the Spanish controls, only to be waved straight through into no-man's-land. Vehicles are then ushered into the shabby Moroccan frontier station, where an atmosphere of unmitigated chaos and disorder prevails. Vehicles are scattered around, some being searched and others just waiting. Dozens of people can be seen running, queuing or shouting, while armed guards bark incomprehensible instructions in a vain attempt to restore an order which probably never existed.

You should find your way to the passport office, and obtain vehicle importation permits. Do not be afraid to return to the office to check that the passports are making progress. Otherwise you can easily while away several hours passively awaiting their emergence from the small window. After a succession of officials arrive and begin to examine your papers, only, it would appear, to lose interest halfway through, you will face your final passport check before being waved on through.

Welcome to Morocco!

Ceuta to Tetouan

The P28 begins its 42 km southward journey to the town of Tetouan by clinging to the Mediterranean coast. During the summer months (and also the month of Ramadan), the beaches are scattered with the colourful and varied tents of native holidaymakers. Scruffy children often emerge from them and run up to the road, gazing in bemusement at passing Land Rovers.

This part of the coastline in peppered with official campsites – Moroc-Tourist and Club Méditerranée. After the purgatory of the border crossing, it is very tempting to make your own first stopover on these inviting dunes. If you do stay outside the official compounds, precautions are absolutely essential. There is a natural tendency for inexperienced campers to push their belongings to the edge of their tents and sleep in the middle. This lends a sense of entirely false security. During the night you may hear a rustling, only to dismiss it as a gentle breeze or the sound of the waves lapping on to the shore. However, the following morning may reveal that a practised team has run a razor blade around the circumference of your tent. Conveniently placed baggage can then be removed and saleable commodities – cameras, personal stereos, clothing and money – rifled from them. The initial panic of having lost one's passport is often shortlived, however, as they will often be found piled together a few yards from your camp.

Even so, this stretch of coast is a pleasant location for a short rest. You can excite phosphorescence as you splash about in the warm sea, while looking out for the groups of moth-eaten camels that are occasionally herded across the sands. Despite their ragged appearance, these are photogenic creatures. They are quite willing to stop and be stroked and filmed, with only the occasional rasping growl. Steer clear of the back end, though!

Leaving the rapidly growing tourist developments, the road heads inland as it approaches Tetouan. (As it does so, look out for storks who make their nests on disused towers and minarets.) The town has an impressive position, and is quite attractive. The architectural style will not be unfamiliar if you have driven through the Moorish areas of southern Spain en route to Morocco. The 1-star Hotel Regina in the Rue Sidi Mandri is acceptable if you need to stay in the town. However, the proximity to the coast means that accommodation may be scarce in the summer months. If your time is short, then the attractions of the medina can be foregone in anticipation that Fes is soon to follow. The visitor to Tetouan should be aware that this town is renowned for the number of hashish-peddlars that plague the visiting tourist. As always, a firm but courteous refusal is the best response.

Crossing the Rif Mountains

Leaving Tetouan, the P28 heads for Chechaouen, 60 km away. As you move further south and further inland, the humidity and morning mists of the coast are steadily replaced by an arid and punishing heat. The landscape begins as a mildly undulating panorama of parched earth and olive-green scrub.

Nonetheless, this road crosses some of Morocco's most productive agricultural land. It is cultivated (without machinery) by isolated farming communities. You will see large circular heaps of grain being threshed at the sides of the road. A team of four or five horses are hitched together in a line. The farmer wields a length of rope as he urges them to trample knee-deep through the grain, in order to remove the chaff. The process seems like a grotesque parody of animals performing in a circus.

Further away from the road, goats and sheep can be seen grazing the scarce vegetation.

After 30 km or so, a small minor road leads off to the right. This takes you to the Souk-el-Arba-des-Beni-Hassan. This is worth a look if you pass through on a Wednesday, as you will find the main market for one of the nineteen Berber tribes that inhabit the area around the Rif. The road passes straight through and rejoins the P28 a couple of kilometres to the south. Back on the main road, you can see the 1,900 m Jbel Kelti rising up to your left. After a further 15 km, the P39 branches away on the left and leads to Chechaouen.

Chechaouen is tucked away in the foothills of the Rif, only becoming visible as you enter it. This is explained by the settlement's original role – as a secret military base. The town has a population of under 20,000, and can be explored without great difficulty. Rough-camping can be avoided in one of the town's pensions, or by using the official site on the hillside.

Continuing beyond Chechaouen on the P39, you will be brought back to the P28. (The best views of the town are from the road leaving to the south.) The next 10 km take you into the Jebala Mountains – a twisting route through rugged terrain. The road then follows the gorge of the Oued Loukos for some of its winding journey to the Atlantic. Slow, careful driving for 40 km bring you into Ouezzane, a holy town for both Islam and Judaism. The settlement is memorable more for its position than its contents, although the octagonal minaret, with its green decoration, is quite impressive.

Beyond Ouezzane, the P26 climbs high into the rarefied atmosphere of the Rif. The Rif is the northernmost of Morocco's major mountain ranges. Ouezzane lies at the western end of their 300 km sweep. Further to the east, this limestone backbone reaches a maximum height of 2,500 m. Perched high in the majestic scenery is a small café (about 30 minutes out of Ouezzane). The colourfully tiled terrace is a delightful vantage point from where to admire the view. As you do so, try a dish of spicy chicken with day-glo saffron rice, washed down with cold drinks or hot, sweet mint tea.

Examination of a map will show that the (apparently) more direct P26 to Fes is some 20 km longer than the more westerly route which follows the P28/P3. Nonetheless, confident and fairly adventurous drivers may well prefer the former route. Viewed from the twisting and often precipitous road, the vistas are quite breathtaking. This journey should not be rushed, even if that were possible! Nonetheless, be sure to stock up with mineral water before you leave the café. The liquid will be unpleasantly warm within minutes, but any relief from the stifling atmosphere is welcome.

There are very few villages en route that are of sufficient size to boast a café. However, at one road junction, in the middle of nowhere, you come across a row of corrugated iron huts. These sell water, drinks and some food. The sight of the fridges lurking in these huts seems to promise welcome refreshment. Do not be fooled – the nearest electricity supply is tens of miles away!

The next 70 km carry you across the final set of Rif foothills, to the tiny Fes-el-Bali. Following a series of hairpins, the road curves around the base of Jbel Amergou. On its slopes stand the remains of a wall, built in the eleventh century. The journey reaches its highest point 30 km later at the Sebou Pass. The final approach into Fes is a spectacular sight. As you wind down from the mountains. Fes is stretched out below in the Saiss plain, with the Middle Atlas providing a distant backdrop. Olive plantations surround the city. This descent is most impressive in the evening, when nerves are tightened by negotiating the bends in the dark, and the lights of the erstwhile imperial capital are arrayed below you.

Fes

Introduction

The city of Fes almost defies description through the written word. It bombards the senses and hijacks the emotions. Even the most crowded itinerary should leave aside two or three days to obtain a taste of this wonderful place.

Although its origins date from some years earlier, the first major impetus of development for Fes began in the ninth century. This occurred under the influence of Idriss II, who made it his capital city. Over the succeeding centuries, Fes vied with Marrakech for royal favour. Much of its enduring influence stemmed from the role played by the Quaraouyine University, which even predates those of Bologna, Oxford and Paris. The French declared Fes to be an 'historical monument'. Paradoxically, this preserved the city, while divesting it of much of its life and purpose. In modern times, the dominance of Rabat has almost entirely destroyed the remaining Fassi influence. The city is increasingly forced to rely upon tourism and the production of craftwork.

While you explore Fes, it is best to base yourself in the official campsite, even if you are aiming to rough camp wherever possible. As with all large settlements, you may have to stay an inconvenient distance from the centre if you try to go it alone. In addition, by avoiding the perimeter, you can be reasonably sure that vehicles and belongings will be safe, as armed guards patrol the compound. The Camping Moulay Slimane is within easy walking distance of the centre of the New Town. It stands on the Rue Moulay Slimane, which branches off the Avenue Youssef Ben Tachfine. If you have difficulty locating it, hail a passing motorcyclist, who may well guide you there for a couple of dirhams. The site offers a swimming

A Fes bakery

pool, toilet/shower facilities of a sort and pleasant café. The site is also quite close to a mosque, which means that you are well in earshot of the muezzin's amplified early-morning call to prayer.

Exploring the city

There are many excellent guidebooks to Fes, and general texts on Morocco rightly devote several pages to the city. Consequently, we will not attempt to provide an exhaustive description here. The visitor with limited time in the city is probably best advised not to wander around with guide-book in one hand and map in the other. The best strategy is almost certainly to employ a guide to give you a general tour, leaving you free to return to areas which particularly interest you. A quick visit to the camp-site office will almost certainly provide a suitable candidate.

You should bear in mind that the guides are generally in the pay of a number of assorted craft sellers, and you will thus be taken to see their wares. This is a perfectly pleasant way to see the city, but it is useful to have a few non-commercial places which you can ask to visit as well.

Fes can be divided into three broad zones, beginning with the New Town built by the French. You may well decide to stay there, but there is little to see. The adjacent area of Fes-el-Jdid (which confusingly means 'Fes the New') is dominated by the palace of the Merenids, which was built in the late thirteenth century. The most interesting area is Fes-el-Bali, which lies on the opposite side of Fes-el-Jdid from the New Town. This astonishing mini-city was established in the ninth century. Even the briefest exploration will reveal sights and sensations impossible to forget.

It is worth beginning your tour with a visit to the Merenid tombs. These fourteenth century ruins are unremarkable in themselves, but their location affords the best overall panorama of the city. The three parts of Fes are easy to distinguish in the basin below. Unfortunately, photography is often hindered by the dusty haze, as well as the sheer scale of the view. The buildings of Fes-el-Bali lie in a chaotic jumble, contrasting with the scrub-speckled hills beyond. The skyline is punctuated by the minarets of Fes's 275 mosques– the highest and holiest being dedicated to Moulay Idriss. The green tiles of the Quaraouyine Mosque proclaim its privileged royal status.

After gazing down on acres of roofs, it is interesting to move on to one of the city's potteries, where you will be able to see tiles, pots and plates being shaped, dried and fired. The roofing tiles are now moulded on a block of wood, but their design originates from the practice of shaping the wet clay around the potter's leg. Many thousands can be seen stretched out on the flat roof, drying in the scorching heat. The imperfect tiles are broken up and used to make mosaics, often with the blue/green colouring characteristic of Fes. Children of six or seven can be seen working here, most of them living on site.

When you come to explore the main medina area, the vehicles are best left with a guardian, whose team of youths will protect them for a few dirhams. If you are being escorted around, then take care to keep in contact with the guide. Always be sure to know the name of the place where the vehicles are left, then if you do become lost, you can always employ a boy to show you the way back. (Guides will often tell you that the medina is dangerous. This is an exaggeration designed to make their services seem more indispensable.)

The first thing to impress itself upon the visitor to the medina is the pungent collection of smells – donkey slurry, spices, dyes, curing leather, foods and bustling humanity. This large walled area of hilly, narrow, cobbled streets is a constant hive of activity. Small boys rush up and offer you ice-cream or slabs of fudge – both best avoided. Cries of 'Barak!' warn you when a heavily laden donkey is being urged along to your rear. You must quickly find a doorway or a recess into the wall in order to get out of the way. In days gone by, Fes-el-Bali was such a thriving commercial centre that visiting Arab traders had to leave their donkeys at a hostel on the perimeter.

Nowadays trade has declined, but the angry buzz of a recklessly driven moped is still about the only concession to the twentieth century.

You will pass a variety of fascinating shops. Look out for the chemists. They sell a vast range of peculiar herbs, together with assorted powders and potions of various colours. Among the curative curiosities are eye of newt and snakes' teeth – available without prescription!

Walking through the medina, you will see a succession of small children carrying flat, circular loaves or pieces of dough. These are being taken to or from one of Fes-el-Bali's bakeries. It is not actually possible to purchase bread here. Instead, families pay a small sum to bring their own dough for baking, coming back to collect it some hours later.

If possible, try to visit the Andalous mosque. Like all mosques in Morocco, non-Moslems are not permitted entry. Nonetheless, the imposing entrance. gate is an impressive sight. The gate is intricately carved, with a classic horseshoe shape. The edifice is topped by an overhanging cedarwood roof. Unusually, this mosque (which was built for immigrant Arabs from Andalucia) catered for both men and women.

Close by is the disused Sarija medressa. A medressa is the Quaraouyine equivalent of an Oxbridge college. Part of the teaching would take place here, as well as the housing of some of the university students. Built in the fourteenth century, it is presently undergoing restoration.

The medressa is an astonishing architectural spectacle. Passing through the main gate, you enter a rectangular atrium with a shallow, blue-tiled pool in the centre. This was originally used for ritual cleansing. Around the edge are a series of intricately carved panels. These served to separate the sexes – they now give the atrium a cloistered effect. Behind the screens are ceramic tiles and stuccoed walls. Like the cedarwood screens, their decoration is a complex and involved combination of swirls and geometric designs. On the other side of the pool from the gate lies the 'mihrab', which indicates the direction of Mecca. The wood surrounding it is stained with mint, henna and saffron. By climbing up a set of stairs to the first floor, you can look into the tiny cells in which the students were accommodated. For thirteen years, young men would stay here and study the Koran. It was not unusual for them to become mad and die in the process. Climbing the ladder on to the roof, you look down on to an adjacent cemetery which stands as testament to this. The view from here is quite eerie. You are raised above the bustle and stench at ground level. Beyond the green tiles of the medressa, the shabby white and brown buildings extend into the distance, with the somehow anachronistic sight of television aerials punctuating the skyline.

Leaving the medressa, you can walk back past the Andalous mosque, and then along the Rue Seftah. This leads down to the Bein el Moudoun bridge. The fast-flowing torrent beneath is little more than an open sewer for the city.

A few yards away, on the other side if the bridge, lies one of the most remarkable sights in Fes – the Tanneries. An iron stomach is a vital prerequisite for a visit! The stench is quite incredible. The skins are first soaked in water, and any remaining flesh is then scraped away. They are then cured in cow's urine before the dyeing takes place, in a large courtyard. A series of round stone vats are filled with liquid dyes. The tanners take the skins and then trample

The Fes tanneries with drying skins on the roof tops

them in the vat. They wash regularly, but their legs are still permanently stained and vulnerable to skin cancer. Once coloured, the skins are carried up to the roofs of surrounding buildings, where they dry in the sun.

We noted above that guides are likely to take you to salesmen with whom they have pre-arranged deals. One of the most likely is the state-run carpet co-operative. Haggling is not permitted for the standard carpets, but the salesmen will soon spot those who are susceptible to a special deal. A visit to the co-operative is a wonderful introduction to Moroccan sales skills at their finest.

As you enter from the street, the cool, dark central chamber is a welcome contrast to the sweltering heat outside. The building was constructed in the nineteenth century, as a house for an astronomer. The main hall is a square, with sides about 25 ft in length. Looking upwards, you will see that it is over 60 ft in height. Small shafts of sunlight show that it was originally open to the sky, but has now been covered by slats. Intricate multicoloured mosaics cover the columns which rise up in the corners of the chamber. The high walls are covered with beautiful old patterned carpets, which hang like tapestries.

Guests/visitors/victims are seated on marble benches, flush to the walls. Food and drink are then bought out. The drink, as so often, is mint tea. Piping hot water is poured on to leaves of mint and lots of sugar, in delightful silver teapots. This is then poured (from a height of 18in or so) into thick glass tumblers. This is delicious, and quite harmless. The same cannot be said for the chilli and goatmeat kebabs. Eating one of these is an undoubted victory for the spirit of adventure, over the rational desire for intestinal stability!

As you eat, drink and enjoy the atmosphere, the selling begins. A master of ceremonies explains the intricacies of the different standards of carpet (based on the number of stitches per sq. m) As he does so, a succession of beautiful examples (often in the characteristic blue of Fes) are flamboyantly displayed on the square marble floor. Many of these have taken a single weaver six months or so to create. You may begin determined to leave with wallet intact – the spirt may be willing, but the credit card is weak. For those obviously too penurious to afford the £500 or so that is often demanded, a display of woven rugs is offered in an ante-chamber. For these, haggling is permitted. The visiting European, however, is no match for native skills. Each sale is greeted by a round of applause, cheering and invocated blessing for a long and successful life. The lucky purchaser is physically dragged to the cash-desk, before doubts and second-thoughts have time to germinate.

Leaving the co-operative with finances depleted, you may feel that you have learned a lesson. However, on sober reflection, hours spent later with the metal-workers, leather-workers and djellabah-makers will convince you otherwise.

It is worth reiterating again – a visit to the living time-capsule of Fes-el-Bali is an experience that will not easily be forgotten. If at all possible, it should be made part of any Moroccan itinerary.

The Middle Atlas

Fes to Azrou

The direct route

The quickest way to get from Fes to the town of Azrou is to follow the P24 south for 80 km. The first few kilometres take you across the remainder of the Fes plain. Before long the road begins a gradual climb through scrubland, where rocky outcrops stick up through the brown grasses. It is well worth stopping for a while and taking a close look in the vegetation. A number of animal species will be found: dragonflies, snakes, scorpions and a plethora of crickets and grasshoppers. One of the more amazing inhabitants is a black millipede, often about 20 cm in length.

As the road crosses the plain, look out for large, black Berber tents, which are scattered across the wilderness. These 'khaima' have a high central ridge, with the canvas pegged quite some distance horizontally, so that the roof has a surprisingly shallow slope.

About 40 km from Fes, the P24 passes through Immouzer-du-Kandar. This is a popular spot for native tourists from Fes. The main attraction of this town, as a resort, lies a few kilometres further along the main road – the lake of Dayet Aouya. There are also some curious dwellings, which have been hewn out of the rock.

The 25 km south to Ifrane bring you through an increasingly green landscape. This is the fringe of the cedar forests, which climb up the slopes of the Middle Atlas peaks. Ifrane itself is a modern settlement, constructed by the French earlier this century. During winter this is an important ski-centre, based around an old volcanic crater. There is little of interest during the summer months.

Leaving Ifrane, Azrou lies 17 km to the south-west.

An alternative route – via Volublis, Moulay Idriss and Meknes

This journey is considerably longer than the run down the P24. In fact, at over 160 km, it is more than twice the distance. As compensation, it will take you through three of Morocco's most famous, and most visited, tourist traps. The route will only be dealt with briefly here, as the standard guide-books give this area a perfectly adequate coverage.

Take the P1 west out of Fes for 10 km, and then turn right on to the P3. You will come 30 km later to Nzala-des-Beni-Ammar. Turn left here, on to the picturesque S306. This twists its way through the olive groves for 17 km, until it joins the P28.

Voulblis lies a very short distance to the north, on the other side of the road. The remarkably well-preserved ruins are remnants of the prosperous capital of a Roman province. Civilisation here, though, predates direct Roman rule. There is evidence of the influence of Carthage (just outside present-day Tunis) in the third century BC. This area provided many animals for the entertainment of Roman citizens in the arena. The ruins are dominated by the main public buildings, although houses, temples and mosaics can all be seen.

Moulay Idriss lies about 4 km south on the P28, on the opposite side of this large, productive valley. This is a holy city for Islam, and infidels are not allowed to stay here overnight. Religious restrictions means that sight-seeing is limited for the non-Moslem, but the situation is most impressive. The city was founded (and named after) one of the great-grandsons of the prophet Mohammed. Moulay Idriss was a great religious figure, as well as being the first of the Alid rulers of Morocco.

Leaving Moulay Idriss, you continue south along the P28 for about 8 km. At the junction with the P6, turn left and Meknes lies 10 km to the south.

At an altitude of over 520 m, Meknes lies at the bottom of the Little Atlas. Favourable natural conditions encouraged the Meknassa Berbers to establish a settlement here in the tenth century. The city owes much of its prosperity and success to Moulay Ismail, who established his capital here in the early eighteenth century. Once again, we find a preponderance of green-tiled roofs, which indicate royal patronage. The medina is worth exploring, as is the Palace complex.

From Meknes, the P21 heads south-east towards Azrou, 62 km away. Initially the road follows the course of the Oued Boufekrane. The major settlement en route, El-Hajeb, was originally occupied by cave-dwellers. About two-thirds of the way from El-Hajeb to Azrou, there is a panorama to the right of the road. From an altitude of 1,400 m you gaze over the remarkable Paysage d'Ito. The river basin of the Oued Tigriga is covered with curious mounds, against a backdrop of mountains.

Azrou

Azrou's position, at the centre of a communication network, ensures that this is a bustling market town. (The main souk is on Tuesdays.) Handicraft production is particularly well-known here. Despite its attractions, to explore the Middle Atlas at their best, you really want to be based in the wilderness. Nonetheless, Azrou is a good centre in which to stock up with petrol, water and other provisions.

The Cedar Forests

Getting there

Leaving Azrou to the south-west, you should follow the P24 for 19 km. (This will be signposted for Khenifra.) Just beyond the small settlement of Tiouririne, the minor S303 leads off to the left. Thirteen kilometres south along this road, you will come to Ain Leuh. This large Berber village is typical of settlements in the Middle Atlas. Moroccan bargaining skills may again come into evidence here. Tourists with large vehicles can soon find themselves agreeing to sell surplus fuel for well below the market price.

The cedar forest of the Middle Atlas

The area to the south of Ain Leuh contains many spots suitable for rough camping. Large clearings in the cedars give plenty of room for tents, while still providing welcome shade. Try to avoid building open camp-fires in the forest, as the police can be very touchy about it.

The forests of the Middle Atlas

The Atlas or Atlantic cedar is a different species to the more familiar Lebanon cedar. In the Middle Atlas they tend to form thick, homogeneous forests. This means that they are usually not as large or as awe-inspiring as those which grow in isolation. The trees begin life with sharp, pointed tops. With the passage of time, the elements conspire to create the classic truncated profile. Occasionally you come across the rarer blue cedar. These forests are unique. They stretch through a wilderness of mountains, sadly crossed by few passable tracks.

This part of the Middle Atlas is a superb base for the naturalist. Several habitats each support a wide range of animals and plants. First, there are the cedars. These are often so dense that little else is able to grow. In areas where they have been felled for their timber, however, flowers provide nectar for myriads of insects. Second, there are large grassland zones between the tracts of forest. Careful examination shows that some of these are deep, wide bowls. These valley-like areas are dolines. Over thousands of years, water action forms underground caverns in the limestone. If the roof of the cavern collapses, a doline is formed on the surface. There are many such dolines in the Middle Atlas, some of them several kilometres across. As a result of the steep sides, some invertebrates, such as small moths and butterflies, become isolated in the larger dolines. Over many years of isolation, they develop different physical characteristics (size and colour) from the populations outside the dolines.

A wide variety of plants and creatures live among the patches of cedar and limestone outcrops. One of the most impressive species is the armoured Rhinocerous beetle. Its orange-brown head is scattered with black lumps, while the colouring is reversed on the abdomen – shiny black segments are spotted with a grid of orange blotches. The campsite area is also home to the vast millipedes found to the south of Fes, as well as lurking scorpions and nocturnal tarantulas. These species are quite small in comparison with their infamous relatives of the same name. Generally speaking, you will only come into contact with scorpions if you actively search for

The large crawling cricket of the Middle Atlas

them – under large stones and fallen logs. Look out for a large species of cricket in the forest. Four or five centimetres in length, it is
black with numerous orange and white spots.

Brambles grow in clearings and by the roadside. During midsummer they provide a valuable source of nectar for butterflies and
moths. Most noticeable are the hummingbird hawk moths. They
take up the nectar with a long proboscis, which means that they do
not have to land. In addition, there are large fritillaries, festoons,
and striped and Moroccan graylings. *Xylocopa violacea*, a large-
bodied black bee, with brown wings, is another fan of the nectar.

It is interesting to note the ways in which the animal inhabitants of the Middle Atlas have adapted to cope with the heat.
Certain species of snail have evolved white shells. The cicadas,
whose rhythmic chirrupping provides a constant aural backdrop to
campsite life, spend some fifteen years underground during their
larval stage.

Fossils are widespread in the loose limestone outcrops. The Atlas
mountains were once part of the seabed, so it is relatively easy to
find fossil bivalves such as scallops and cockles. Trilobites and
ammonites are not as easy to locate, but the children in Ain Leuh
and other villages often have them for sale or barter. There are
many opportunities to buy fossils from street vendors, for example,
at Midelt.

The macaque monkey that inhabits the cedar forest

Heading south from the campsite, you may well catch a fleeting glimpse of some macaque monkeys (*Macaca inuus*). These are related to the famous barbary apes of Gibraltar. The Middle Atlas is their last remaining wild habitat. They are solidly built, with long faces and large shoulders. Macaques live in troops of up to twenty individuals. They wander through the forests looking for food on the ground. They are very shy creatures and if disturbed will quickly climb into the cedars. We have seen them on several occasions, crossing the road just beyond the suggested camp area.

As you move south, the cedars progressively thin out. The road climbs on to a ridge. Beyond this, a series of low, black Berber tents can be seen. Between the tents, the Berbers sink wells to provide themselves with water. Flocks of sheep roam around them.

Lake Ouiounane lies about 20 km from Ain Leuh. This small, eutrophic (nutrient-rich) lake has thick aquatic vegetation. It supports a wide variety of invertebrates, especially dragonflies. Tree frogs and terrapins abound, as do numerous small guppy-like fish. The water is unsuitable for drinking.

Having passed through an area of spectacular mountain scenery, you come upon an elegant terraced village, with storks nesting among the rooftops. (The children here are very eager to act as photographic models – for a small consideration!)

Just over 30 km south of the campsite, the road crosses the Oumer Rbia river. Vehicles can be left here (preferably accompanied) while you walk along to the source of the river, and the famous cascades. It has to be said that these are not as breathtaking as many guides make them out to be. Nonetheless, the opportunity for a refreshing swim and wash is most welcome. This is the only source of drinking water in the area other than buying mineral water in Ain Leuh. Even here, the Moroccan trading instinct is not absent. On our last visit, aspirins and the cotton sheets used to cover the seats of the Land Rover were both valued commodities.

As well as affording an opportunity for relaxation, the cascade area will be of interest to the naturalist. Oleander is the dominant vegetation, while animal life includes dragonflies, frogs, toads, fish and, surprisingly, a species of freshwater crab.

Azrou to Midelt

Having travelled some 50 km away from Azrou, it may seem rather a waste of time to retrace your steps before continuing south. The maps appear to indicate that rough tracks leave the S303 from a couple of kilometres to the south of Ain Leuh. They cross rough ground before emerging on the P21, 15 or 20 km south of Azrou.

You should only contemplate attempting this route if you have a robust four-wheel-drive vechicle. The landscape is strewn with boulders and provides a very bumpy ride. Amidst the rocks and scrub, the track often proves difficult to follow as it splits, merges or almost disappears. After all, the route is merely the collected tyre imprints of the last ten or so vehicles to attempt the crossing. Do not be fooled into the impression that tyre marks imply a traversable journey. Landslips or rockfalls mean that a previously well-used route can terminate abruptly with a wall of boulders or a narrow precipice. If you do find yourself fooled by the tracks, look out for the intermittent piles of rocks which are the best guides to the direction of civilisation. Finally, if in doubt, there is no shame in admitting defeat and retreating to the S303.

Returning to Azrou, you then head south on the P21 for approximately 100 km.

Initially, the road rises in altitude as it makes its way through the cedar forest. Leaving the trees behind, your journey continues through an impressive region of barren plains, with a view of some of the highest mountains of the Middle Atlas. Thirty-two kilometres to the south of Azrou, the P21 passes through Timahdite and runs parallel to the Oued Guigou river – a good stretch of water for fishing. The roadside is littered with black rocks. These lumps of pumice are characteristic of this type of volcanic plateau. Once again, the black tents of the Berber shepherds are a common feature of the area away from the road. Black kites can often be seen circling above them.

Just over 50 km south of Azrou there is a turning left off the P21 to the Aguelmane Sidi Ali. One kilometre down this track (the S332), you emerge at the shore of a large lake, with a range of cedar-scattered hills on the far side. The lake is at an altitude of 2,000 m, and was formed in a crater of volcanic rocks. There are several such lakes in this region, but at 3 km in length, this is the largest. You are very unlikely to meet anyone else in this spot, so it is a good place to stop for a while. As well as being an attractive and peaceful area, there is plenty for the naturalist. The most obvious sign of life is the carpet of locusts which covers the ground near the water. As you walk beneath the fierce sun, your footsteps stir up little flurries of the creatures around you. Away from the flat, open plain, it is not difficult to spot toads, lizards and scorpions. In addition, the lake is an abundant source of pike, trout and other fish. Where evaporation has caused the edges of the lake to recede,

The lake of Sidi Ali

an area of sand has been revealed. This is inhabited by narrow-waisted black and red solitary wasps. These dig small burrows in the sand. After paralysing their prey (spiders and insect larvae), the wasps leave the immobilised food in the burrow, with a single egg attached.

Moving further south from Sidi Ali, the P21 traverses the vast Plateau de l'Arid. This is an area of lowland between the Middle and High Atlas. The drive across this plain, to Midelt, is at its most breathtaking in the late afternoon. As the heat haze subsides, the vast mountains rise up in a sheer golden backdrop to the town. The Jbel Ayachi Range reaches over 3,700 m in altitude.

The town of Midelt itself is nothing to write home about. Sitting in one of the few cafés you will soon be pestered by eager salesman, trying to dispose of hashish, minerals and fossils. The Atlas ranges contain some of the finest trilobite deposits in the world. Small, chalky examples are available for a few pence. Most impressive is a 10–15 cm, jet-black fossil called phacops. One of the largest species of trilobite, it lived in the oceans 550 million years ago. A genuine phacops fossil can be quite expensive. Although you will find stalls in Meski and on the way to Marrakech, we found Mildelt to be the cheapest place to buy fossils. Cassettes of Western music are a good item to barter for large, beautifully polished Ceratites – a fossil that developed late in the history of the ammonites.

If you have a couple of hours to kill, there is an interesting selection of carpets available in the old souk.

The South-East

The Ziz Gorge

Having left Midelt, the P21 winds up into the High Atlas. As it does so, the traveller is treated to some superb scenery. In addition to the bare mountainsides themselves, you should look out for picturesque basaltic extrusions. Beautiful geological patterns have been created as hot rock has emerged from the earth's crust, cooling on the surface.

The crossing has its highest point some 30 km from Midelt. The Tizi-n-Talrhemt (or 'Pass of the She-Camel') – is at an altitude of 1,907 m. This is one of the lowest crossing points in the range. Once over the pass, the road descends on to a barren desert plain. After 45 km or so, a small road leads off to the right. Within a couple of kilometres, you enter the town of Rich. There is little to keep you here, except the opportunity to restock supplies of water and petrol. As you do so, there will be time to admire the mountain panorama stretched before you. During the evening, the rock is washed with a glorious shade of reddy-orange.

Continuing southwards, the main road shadows the Ziz river as it meanders its way into the desert. The river is often almost dry in the summer months. The wide bed, though, bears testament to the powerful and destructive surges which occasionally occur. Twenty-four kilometres from Rich, the P21 disappears into the 'Legionaires' Tunnel'. As you emerge from the tunnel, you find yourself in the remarkable Ziz Gorge. For a 20 km stretch, the road follows a breathtaking canyon – hewn out of the Atlas by the erosive power of an often feeble-looking river.

Almost immediately after leaving the tunnel, you can see the gorge sweeping round from right to left. With care you can drive down from the road, and on to the area of river-bed on the inside of the curve. The ground has a fairly flat covering of dried alluvial mud. This is quite good for supporting tents. You will need some form of cushioning to sleep on, as, in time, small pebbles have a tendancy to make their presence felt through the soft sediment.

Understandably, the harsh conditions severely limit the range of vegetation which is able to survive. Leafless thorn bushes dominate, supported by tough fibrous cells. Islands of oleander are to be found on the river bed. As the course is often almost dry, the oleander relies on its deep tap roots to collect water. Tamarisk grows in dense thickets. The thorn bush, *zizyphus*, is found further away from the water.

None of the animal life is obvious. Look out for minute black and white butterflies – little more than a centimetre in length. These are a form of tiger blue (genus *Tarucus*). They live in a number of localities but are normally associated with large *zizyphus* bushes. So small are these butterflies that they spend most of their lives within the air spaces of the bush, only emerging when in search of a mate. Their larvae feed on the thorn bushes. Small holes in the ground, with mounds of earth beside them, are the dwellings of antlion larvae. These are tiny hunchbacked predators. Somewhat larger, and certainly more vocal, are the large numbers of green frogs.

One of the most interesting inhabitants of the Ziz Gorge is the *galeodes* (or wind scorpion). The common name arises because of the creature's phenomenal speed. Although a close relative of the scorpion it does not have a sting. It also boasts the largest set of jaws (relative to its own size) in the animal kingdom. These two facts demand some caution if you attempt to capture any specimens. The most important precaution, when looking under a rock, is to first lift up the side furthest away from your body. If you do this, any startled creatures will not be forced to run straight

The fertile Ziz Gorge

towards you. The Ziz Gorge is one of the first opportunities to see these remarkable small creatures, although the larger, more formidable varieties are found much further south. They are common throughout the Sahara.

As well as animals and plants, the massive rock and scree slopes are also a fruitful source of fossils. The high slopes on the other side of the river can be climbed within half an hour. There is a superb view from the top.

Although this northern section of the Ziz Gorge is an interesting area to visit, it is also far from hospitable. For much of the day, the heat at the bottom of this vast rock basin is almost unbearable.

Driving steadily further south along the Ziz Gorge, you will find your journey frequently interrupted by a succession of photo-stops. One stretch, reproduced on a thousand post-cards and tourist posters, enables you to look down on a panorama of tall palms and greenery, filling the floor of the gorge and surrounding the shallow river which runs through it.

Leaving this fertile valley behind, the P21 then moves through a region of extensive canyon, enormous scree slopes and a dramatic geology of folded rock strata. To the left is the expanse of the Hassan Addakhil reservoir. This was created in the early 1970s, when the Ziz was dammed in order to control its flow and provide irrigation for the region.

Beyond the reservoir lies the sprawling town of Er Rachidia.

The Oasis of Meski

The town of Er Rachidia is less than 15 years old. It was constructed by the French as a centre of regional administration and as a garrison town. The military presence is explained by the proximity of the border with Algeria, and the activities of the Polisario – a guerrilla group with Algerian support, who seek the independence of the former Spanish territories in the Sahara.

Er Rachidia has a functional, modern and prosperous feel to it. Given its position, this seems to lend a curious air of artificiality. If you intend to spend some time in the south, it is wise to change a fair amount of money here, as banks are naturally scarce in the less populous areas. A further attraction of the bank is the superb airconditioning. After a sweltering drive from the Ziz Gorge, half an hour in the cool and luxurious foyer of the Banque Populaire is most welcome. Beyond this, and the customary sojourn in a local café, there is little to detain you here.

The oasis of Meski surrounded by the Reg desert, with the High Atlas on the horizon

You should head east from Er Rachidia on the P32. Running parallel to the river Ziz, the road leads out on to the desert plateau. The desert here is not the sea of sand familiar from *Beau Geste* or *Lawrence of Arabia*. Instead, it is a type of desert known as 'reg'. The wind has blown the loose sand away from the flat plain, leaving a desolate moonscape of gravel, pebbles and small rocks.

Eighteen kilometres from Er Rachidia, the P21 leaves the main road on the right, continuing to shadow the Ziz. The junction is also marked by a small sign for the 'Source Bleue de Meski'. A track takes you down from the desert plateau, and into this remarkable oasis – a world within a world.

The camping area is among the young palm trees and tends to be fairly crowded in high season, so large groups may find their tents dispersed throughout the site. Meski's main attraction is a large blue swimming pool, which is fed by a spring (the 'source bleue'). You may well find yourself swimming next to several large fish. The setting of the pool is quite breathtaking. Tall, spiky date palms tower over the water, largely obscuring the sheer rock faces beyond. To one side of the pool, there is a raised terrace which leads on to a restaurant and café. This is a beautiful, but somewhat expensive spot for evening drinks. There are small shops near the camping area. One stocks an impressive range of fossils, including phacops, a large trilobite.

Meski (which means 'an oasis in a depression of stony desert') is a wonderful place for the naturalist to investigate. The oasis is situated in part of the valley of the river Ziz, which extends almost as far south as the Algerian border. The camp is in the centre of the oasis. A particularly rewarding study of the wildlife can be made by walking out of the valley, and slowly climbing up the sides of the gorge to reach the flat plain of the reg-desert above.

In the centre, there is a sluggish and murky stream. This, and the surrounding area of lush vegetation, provides a fertile environment for a wide range of animal species. Beautiful red dragonflies dart across the water, pursuing the millions of mosquitoes which infest the area. The sound of frogs and toads is almost deafening, particularly at night. The frog is a variety of green frog (*Rana ridibunda perezi*). It is the commonest species in this part of Morocco.

The green toad (*Bufo viridis*) is not as common, but it can be found here at Meski and along the line of the Tafilalt oasis. The most spectacular amphibian is the Mauritanian toad (*Bufo mauritanicus*). This large light tan-and-yellow-spotted creature hunts in the palmery of Meski, only occasionally returning to the water. It has the ability to regulate water evaporation from its skin and thereby control (to some extent) its temperature out of the water. A

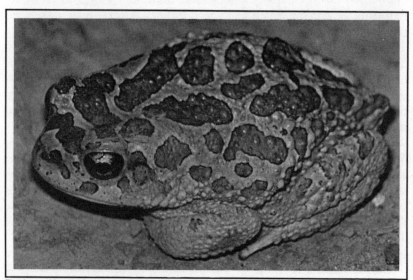

The large, Mauritanian toad to be found in Meski

The Ziz river in the Meski oasis. The kasbah is in the background

sudden rainstorm at night makes them more active and we have discovered them in our tents in the morning! Meski is the only Saharan locality in which the reptile *Mauremys caspica,* a kind of terrapin, is also found.

Frogs and toads are not the only inhabitants of the stream. Terrapins and snakes can also be seen. Unfortunately, it is impossible to make as close a study of the stream as one might wish, because of the danger of bilharzia.The flat bilharzia worm lays eggs which develop into free swimming larvae. These parasites then infect a secondary host – a particular species of snail which is very widespread in and around the stream. Living in the snail, bilharzia develops into another free-swimming form – cercariae. These cercariae infect humans, causing a debilitating disease. Consequently, you should be very careful not to place so much as a foot into the water or the soft mud surrounding it. The key thing to remember is that bilharzia is likely to be a problem in places where water is still or slow-moving. There are rumours that the main pool of Meski is also infected. However, the water comes straight from a spring and does not make contact with the other oasis water. Most importantly, the snails are not present in the pool. Few of the visitors worry about it and all our party used the pool frequently during our last visit, with no one suffering any ill effects.

Climbing up from the centre of the oasis, you can see a large, ruined kasbah. This fort once guarded the approaches to this strategically important area. As you reach the reg, the contrast between the lush oasis and irrigated agricultural plots on the one hand, and the bare desert on the other, is striking. At midday during the summer, the temperature on the open ground often exceeds 40°C. Animal life is restricted to locusts and the desert mantid (*Ermiaphila* sp.). The latter is a well-camouflaged, brown mantid that merges well with the stones. Unlike most varieties, which live in vegetation, this variety is able to move more quickly. With reduced wings and a flattened body, their long, thin legs enable them to move quickly over the reg. Botanists should keep their eyes open for what appears, on first examination, to be a series of small mossy clumps. In fact, these are tiny trees – chou-fleur (*Fredolia aretioides*). They are tightly compacted to avoid water loss.

The Tafilalt

Erg Chebbi

For many visitors to Morocco, their time spent in the Tafilalt is the most memorable of the trip. The desert, the ksours and the palm-

The chou-fleur 'tree' in the Reg desert near Meski

groves are the closest Morocco comes to fulfilling the classic Western expectations of the romantic Sahara. The Tafilalt itself can be roughly defined as the region around the course of the Ziz Valley, from Meski south to Rissani.

As you set off south from the oasis, be prepared for warnings of the dangers lying beyond – from the natural elements and the proximity of the Algerian border. Such tales owe more to the hopes of prospective guides than they do to the presence of any real problems. Obviously, you must be careful when travelling in wilderness areas, but there is little need to hire a guide for any part of our route through the south.

The P21 covers the 60 km from Meski, down to the town of Erfoud. Having climbed up from the depression of the oasis, you travel over a stretch of fairly uninspiring reg. After a few kilometres, the road bears towards the valley itself, between the villages of Zouala and Oulad-Aissa. There are some good vantage-points near here, from which to appreciate the contrast between the pink rocks of the plain, and the dark green of the palmeries below. Progressing further south, keep an eye open for the seven ksour which lie on both sides of the Ziz. These fortified villages were of strategic importance in protecting the trade route from the Mediterranean to Guinea, on the west African coast.

Circling the edge of Erg Chebbi

Also en route to Erfoud, you will catch your first glimpse of an erg – a sandy desert. About 50 minutes' drive from Meski, a relatively small sea of sand rises from the pebbly plain to the west. It is tempting to stop for photographs, but there is little point as the far larger (and more impressive) Erg Chebbi lies just a few hours further on.

With a population of some 5,000 people, Erfoud is a dull, modern market town and administrative centre. A visit to a petrol station (where fuel will normally be hand-pumped), or to one of the cafés, is the only thing to detain you here before moving on. Beware of the sudden gusts of wind that pick up clouds of sand and dust. These strike with surprising speed. Like Meski, Erfoud is a collecting point for hustlers offering to act as guides to the desert.

The road to Merzouga is not well signposted as it leaves Erfoud, so it is well worth asking a local to confirm that you are on the right track. Indeed, after 15 km, 'track' is the operative word. The asphalted road, occasionally covered by drifting sand, gives way to a rough desert piste. (Soon after leaving the town, you will pass some workings which exploit the rich lead deposits of the area.)

Despite its bad condition, the track is relatively easy to distinguish from the landscape around it – reg desert, with rocky outcrops and the occasional tuft of vegetation emerging from it. For certain parts of the journey, it may well be advisable to drive off the established route, in order to avoid the corrugations which can otherwise give you a very bumpy ride. Navigation can be made slightly tricky if you travel during the late afternoon, as there is regularly a strong wind at this time, which can whip up sandstorms. If in doubt, just stay close to the line of telegraph poles that run parallel to the track. They lead all the way to Merzouga.

The spectacular dune system of Erg Chebbi ('Little Sandy Desert') first appears as a golden strip on the eastern horizon. As the track moves closer, the majesty and scale of the desert becomes truly apparent for the first time. A vast, towering ocean of sand rises up from the bare, pebble-strewn plain. Some 40 km from Meski, you will come across a roadside sign for the the Café des Dunes. A track leads off to the left and heads straight for the dunes. The little building is initially hidden from view, behind a small area of sand, separate from the main body of the erg. The tatty concrete café is dwarfed by the huge golden mounds that rise up, just yards in front. A basic construction of wooden slats goes some way to shield you from the sun and sand, as you sit on cushioned benches around the edge of the verandah. The benches also serve as beds,

The café on the edge of Erg Chebbi, from the dunes

although the flat roof is almost as good a place to sleep (and cook). You will find several of these cafés off the Merzouga track.

Surprisingly, you are unlikely to be the only guests in this most isolated of spots. As evening draws in, anything from a camel to a Renault 4 may emerge from the distance. Dinner is often followed by an impromptu musical performance from the owner and a visiting group of Tuaregs. The rhythmic sound of the traditional pottery drums combines with the awesome setting to create a unique atmosphere for the European visitor.

As the sun sets, a brief walk into the dunes will reward you with a sighting of several nocturnal creatures. A torch is essential, as jerboas and fennec foxes are difficult to spot. It is invariably the fresh tracks in the sand that reveal their presence. Beetles abound on the dunes. Common darkling beetles amble about on their spindly legs, while more determined hunters, like the Carabid beetle (*Anthia venator*), move rapidly across the sand and rock. These large carnivorous insects have four white spots on their wing cases, although they are actually flightless. They boast a set of powerful jaws. The desert tenebrionid beetle (*Priontheca coronata*), is a bulky, dark-brown species with numerous spines projecting from all over its body. The wind scorpion lives on the dunes, but, as always, a quick eye is needed to spot them.

The tracks and remains of the meeting of a beetle and a jerboa, Erg Chebbi

For the most magical experience of the desert, though, you will have to wait until early the following morning. Be sure to get up a full hour before dawn, and make your way up and into the massive ocean of sand. The walk is not easy going, but after a while you will find yourself on a ridge of dune, with nothing but sand in every direction, as far as the eye can see. Before the sun has risen, the air and the sand are pleasantly cool. For the following couple of hours, the steady rise in temperature is almost tangible, minute by minute. To wait, surrounded by the enormity and the silence of the Sahara, for the coming dawn, is a breathtaking and unforgettable experience. As the burning golden disc rises over the horizon, the undulating, rippled dunes undergo a magical change of colour — from purple to pink to gold. As they do so, the patterns of shadow change subtly before gradually disappearing as the sun climbs overhead.

Rissani

The town of Rissani lies some three hours' drive from the Café de Dunes. Heading west across one of several sets of established tyre-marks, you will come to the rough piste that leads from just north of Merzouga to Rissani. Although barren and desolate, the landscape on this desert crossing is most impressive. There are occasional patches of vegetation, including desert melons (not to be eaten as they cause vomiting). Fossilised wood is not uncommon in this part of the desert.

Driving conditions are somewhat worse on this route than they are between Erfoud and the dunes. You will often find it easier to drive parallel to, rather than along, the most well-used track. The ride becomes particularly bumpy as you approach Rissani itself. Before reaching the town, the track leads into a large area of dusty, white stone roads, walls and irrigation systems.

Rissani is near the site of Sijilmassa, an eighth-century settlement and stopping-off point for the camel caravans. It is also the point at which the Ziz river finally disappears into the desert. The main reason to visit, though, is the market, which takes place on

The 'camel market' at Rissani

Sundays, Tuesdays and Thursdays. This wonderful souk is housed within the Ksar Abouam. The stalls are shaded beneath arcades topped with slats and palm fronds. Hundreds of people bustle around the vast marketplace. As always, the immediate sensory impact is one of smell. The disparate odours of donkeys, fruit, grain, people and rotting meat all combine in a powerful bouquet. Foodstuffs dominate the centre of the market. Attentive stallholders sit behind massive piles of melons, pumpkins, watermelons and compressed blocks of dates, crawling with flies. Nearby, spice sellers perch beneath tarpaulins suspended from ropes. Their wares are spread about them, in shallow baskets, or in piles on the ground. Around the perimeter of the square are a series of small shops – butchers, carpet-sellers, djellabah salesmen, copper merchants and bookshops. Just beyond the main market place, a large open space is crammed with donkeys for sale. (The Berbers in this region tend to prefer donkeys to camels as they are more economical.)

The High Atlas Gorges

Todra and Dades

The journey from Rissani to the entrance of the Todra Gorge can be comfortably completed in a full afternoon. Head north along the P21 for a little over 20 km. This brings you through the lower reaches of the Tafilalt, and back to Erfoud. From Erfoud, Route 3451 follows the course of the Oued Rheris westwards for 90 km, until it reaches the town of Tinejdad.

Much of this route is an uneventful crossing of 'hamada' (rockplain desert). Visual relief is occasionally provided by a palmery or a few dusty buildings. The last 20 km of the road – between the ksar of Mellab and Tinejdad – passes a relatively verdant oasis. This region is home to the ancient, southern warrior tribe of the Ait Atta. Tinejdad is a good point at which to break the journey. There is a simple little café here, where the owner will spread out cushions and rugs for you as he cooks brochettes over a small fire in the back yard.

Leaving Tinejdad, you join the P32 from Er Rachidia, which traces the 55 barren kilometres to Tinerhir. This is your last chance to refuel before making the journey through the gorges. Although many guide-books tend to dismiss it as little more than a stopping-off point for the gorges, Tinerhir is quite an attractive and interesting place in its own right. As well as facilities, such as a bank and post office, there are a couple of good places to buy carpets. Market day is Monday.

The spectacular scenery of the Todra begins almost as soon as you head north from Tinerhir, along Route 6902. Vast walls of rock rise up from lush valleys of palms and other vegetation, with shallow rivers rushing beneath. The first place where you might consider staying is near the 'Sacred Fish Spring' – a freshwater pool. There is a palmery near the pool, within which lurk a couple of camp-sites. Although this is a delightful spot, even the most hardened camper would be well advised to swallow his or her pride and stay at one of the hotels which stand at the entrance to the gorge's narrowest section.

The hotels lie a little over 5 km further along the road. First is the El Mansour, and then a couple of hundred metres further on, the Hotel des Roches and the Yasmina. Our personal favourite is

Driving through the Todra Gorge

the Hotel des Roches – nestling in an astonishing setting, at the base of the sheer 300 m cliff. There are a few rooms off the main foyer/bar. Even so, it is just as pleasant (and certainly more atmospheric) to sleep beneath the wonderful Berber tent which has been erected adjacent to the main hotel building. Just put a sleeping bag on one of the couches. (If there are other people staying in the hotel, you will obviously have to be wary of leaving personal belongings in the tent.) The food in the hotel is fairly basic, but quite acceptable, although the greasy egg breakfasts are an acquired taste. The cost of staying here is very low, less than a pound a night.

The Oued Todra, which flows along the gorge, just yards from the hotel, is ideal for washing. Watch out in the hours immediately following a cloudburst, as the rushing water can suddenly become dark-brown with disturbed sediment.

The early stretch of the gorge is well worth exploring on foot. Gazing up at the immense walls of rock, barely 60 m apart, can be an awe-inspiring experience. Early evening and early morning are especially beautiful.

A number of caves can be seen in the sides of the gorge. One, close to the hotel, contains the entire population of a unique insect species. They live on the droppings of the bats which also inhabit the cave. Large black crickets are also much in evidence. Be careful when examining them, as they can secrete a repellant, sticky, red fluid. Slightly larger are the lizards and ground squirrels, which can be seen darting into crevices in the rock.

The journey up the Todra Gorge, across the mountains and then down the Dades, should really only be attempted with a sturdy four-wheel-drive vehicle. Having said this, you are bound to come across the odd shabby Renault 4 bouncing its way over the rocky tracks. Even so, it is a brave and confident driver who attempts the route without a Land Rover or equivalent. Initially, the condition of the track is fairly appalling. Drivers should keep a sharp eye out for boulders that have fallen from the slopes above, as well as deceptively deep, mud-filled pot-holes. For much of the first few kilometres, the track is little more than the dry part of a river bed. On occasions, it may even be necessary to stop and 'rebuild' part of the track with nearby rocks and stones. As the river meanders, so vehicles have to ford the river from side to side.

There are at least eight species of lizard and gecko in the gorge. The large black cricket *Eugaster spinulosus* crawls around in the sunshine. The red on the thorax indicates that it is poisonous. It ejects an unpleasant fluid to repel enemies.

In a short while you leave the narrow canyon and the gorge widens out. Massive rugged rock-faces slope downwards to palms and grasses on the valley floor. The angle of slope on the valley sides varies from top to bottom, as the various rock strata erode at different speeds. The differential erosion also means that the golden-brown rock-face often overhangs the track. Patches of oleander colour the landscape, while the desert mantis hunts on the ground.

The road condition improves slightly as you approach Tamtatouchte. The town suddenly appears below, as you reach the brow of a hill, with a truncated mountain rising far beyond it. A rock ridge runs along the edge of the settlement to the right. The flat-roofed buildings are largely made of mud, with grasses and vegetation used for binding and improvised shade. Low walls surround green, irrigated fields of crops. The presence of water also supports

The desert mantis, adapted for fast running

a fair number of palms and other trees. Doorways lead from the road, into small courtyards by each dwelling. Before you reach the first houses, your vehicle will already have been surrounded by a throng of children. Boys with almost shaven heads insistently demand 'un bonbon' or 'un stylo', while their brightly clothed sisters stand back at the edge of the road, staring in bemusement. When you look at the dull brown of the buildings, it is astonishing to see the vibrant colours of the women's clothing. The dyed cloth is often shot through with strands of metallic-blue thread, which shines in the bright sunlight.

Having passed the tall, fortified kasbah, and emerged at the other side of the town, you should take the track up to the left. The route winds up and across a barren yet undulating landscape, with a wonderful panorama of the High Atlas looming up far to the north. The dusty earth is dotted with small, tough clumps of vege-tation. It is interesting to note that they tend to form an almost regular pattern, with gaps of about a metre between each specimen. A number of factors contribute to this phenomenon. Firstly, the lim-ited amount of nutrients and moisture in the soil means that the plants cannot survive too close together. Secondly, some plants are only able to develop in the shade of another. Hence, small plants develop beneath large ones, growing to full size when the older plant dies. Thirdly, some plants secrete biochemical poisons from their root tips, which kill other plants that try to develop nearby. Plants which use this type of defence mechanism are described as being 'oligotrophic'. The spiny plants may be covered with the trailing red stems of parasitic dodder. This is a much thicker species than the European version, but its method of nutrition is the same – to suck out its food from a host plant.

A series of precarious hairpins accompany the steady increase in altitude. At its highest point, the pass reaches 2,800 m. Looking down from this point, the track stretches away – a light stripe across the brown hills. Once the terrain has flattened slightly, there are several good spots at which to consider camping, especially as there are a few streams running through the area. You may, though, need to spend some time clearing the ground of rocks. The rocks in this area (and also further along the Dades) are rich in marine fossils, particularly bivalves.

Understandably, there are few problems of overcrowding here. You may see an intrepid Renault 4, or more likely, a large Bedford truck crammed with people, making its way to Msemir. Perhaps the most likely source of company are the shepherds and goatherds who urge their flocks through this desolate countryside. On our last visit, three young men joined us during the early evening. The eldest amazed us with a surprisingly tuneful rendition from a makeshift violin – constructed from a punctured BP oilcan and a length of wood. He was accompanied by a younger percussionist, beating a rapid rhythm on a plastic bottle.

Keen photographers would do well to rise early in this area, as the canyon is most attractive in the early-morning sunlight. A boulder-strewn scree slope leads up to a series of oblique strata, topped by a jagged ridge. It is also a good idea to break camp before the heat becomes too unbearable. This is also the best time to get out and study the wildlife – look out for large grayling butterflies. These form an interesting contrast with the most common butterfly species in the area, a white variety with a wingspan of barely a centimetre.

Continuing towards the Dades, the vegetation becomes steadily more lush. Stop to investigate one of the meadows and you may come across some unusually large ichneumon wasps. Soon afterwards, you reach the town of Msemir. Like Tamtatouchte, European visitors here are greeted with some curiosity, but if possible, the town certainly merits a leisurely wander.

Descending through the lower Dades Gorge

The Dades Gorge extends for 62 km, south of the high plateau of Msemir. This part of the Route 6901 has been described as the 'Grand Canyon of Morocco', which is hardly an exaggeration. It is astonishing to appreciate the erosive power of the Oued Dades, nestling hundreds of metres below the winding roadway. Small settlements cling to the greenery around the water. It is interesting to note the variety of colours in the substrate – from the austere white of the limestone, to dark reds and greens. Naturally, this is then reflected in the buildings. Basaltic extrusions are another scenic geological feature. As it widens out, the gorge is lined by a large number of kasbahs and ksour, built by chieftains of rival tribes. The scenery also becomes quite verdant, although the mountain climate tends to inhibit the growth of palms.

The drive from Msemir to the junction with the P32 takes a full morning. It is not worth rushing, both because of the careful driving required, and the number of photostops that the incredible scenery demands.

The South-West

The Dades Valley

Back on the P32, Ouarzazate lies 124 km to the south-west. The road follows the valley of the river Dades to a large, dammed lake. Although less noteworthy than the gorge, there are still some interesting sights on this stretch. You join the P32 at the unextraordinary town of Boumalne-du-Dades, with its attractive view over the lush vegetation and impressive kasbah which stand at the entrance to the Dades Gorge. There is a market here on Wednesday – look for the walled compound down the hill. Twenty-four kilometres further on, in the valley of M'Goun, lies El-Kelaa-des-Mgouna. If good fortune brings you to this region during the spring, you will find the wonderful sight of acres of pink Persian roses. The blooms are highly scented, fairly small and grow in hedges. Two factories use the flowers to produce rosewater, for which there is a great demand in Morocco. In May, a festival celebrates the arrival of the year's crop. The oasis here is relatively cool, which has an impact on the plant life. Palms are absent, but almonds and fruit (such as apricots and pomegranates) are common.

After travelling 50 km across a flat plain of semi-desert, you reach Skoura. En route, look out for the roadside stalls from where minerals and fossils are sold. These are generally fairly expensive here, but the knowledgeable may pick up the odd bargain. The village itself is not much to get excited about, although there are some interesting kasbahs nearby. Particularly worth visiting is Amerhidil, which stands 5 km further west. The towers, carved with striking yet intricate geometrical patterns, are most impressive.

Continuing to Ouarzazate, the road leads across semi-desert to the southern slopes of the High Atlas mountains. The town lies at the end of a large lake. Covering four and a half thousand hectares, it has been created by damming the Oued Draa at El-Mansour Eddahbi. The dam is nearly 300 m wide and confines more than half a billion cubic metres of water.

There are a number of fairly cheap hotels in the town. 'Hotel La Vallee' lies a couple of minutes along the road to Zagora. It is a little pricey, but the swimming pool (although little more than 10 ft in length) is fair compensation. The cheapest way to stay is to take a sleeping bag on to the flat roof. At sunset, this also provides a photogenic view back to the town and the hills beyond.

To be frank, there is little to keep you in Ouarzazate, beyond a night's sleep. We found the kasbah here less appealing than the one in Telouet, although the surrounding countryside has attracted the producers of films such as *Lawrence of Arabia*, *Jesus of Nazareth* and *The Living Daylights*. If you find yourself with time to kill in the town, look out for the Ouazguita carpets which are woven by the women of the town. Their characteristic feature is a reddy-orange design on a black background.

Tizi-n-Tichka

The Ascent from Ouarzazate

The P31 from Ouarzazate to Marrakech is the most important of the routes across the High Atlas chain. At slightly over 250 km in length, it is a crucial link from Morocco's major cities to the arid plains and deserts of the south. Driving is relatively easy, as the roads are kept in good condition by the army because of the route's strategic role in providing access to the Algerian border.

Ouarzazate stands at an altitude of 1160 m. The road starts to climb as soon as you leave the town. After 20 km, turn down a track to the right, which will be signposted to Ait Benhaddou. Seven kilometres later you will be confronted by a delightful view of a kasbah to the left of the Asif Mellah (a tributary of the Oued Ouarzazate). It stands on a hillside dominated by ruined fortifications. This wonderful village, with its kasbahs, has appeared as the backdrop to several films. There is no need to retrace your steps to the main road – a track leads off to the left, bringing you back to the P31.

The next few kilometres lead through Imini – a region of manganese mines. The mineral ore is transported by *téléphérique*, the cables of which are occasionally visible from the road. Steadily climbing, the road bears to the right at Agouim. The view to the left at this point gives a panorama of the tallest peaks of the High Atlas. The nearest ridge of mountains reach over 3,800 m in height. Behind them stands Morocco's tallest mountain – Jbel Toubkal – at 4,167 m. A few kilometres later, Irherm-n-Ougdal is worth a visit. This is a typical settlement of the High Atlas. Terraces enable it to occupy its hillside position. The small houses blend in with the natural geology. Look out for the thick-walled, fortified granary, with its slanting tower. Buildings such as this are common in the Atlas. The various floors are divided into small chambers, in which each family in the community could safely store its grain. As well as exploring the village, note that the insect life around here is quite varied. Several streams in the vicinity make the slopes below Irherm a good place in which to replenish water supplies.

At this stage, the journey climbs rapidly to the pass of Tizi-n-Lepsis, at 2,210 m. Almost immediately afterwards Route 6802 winds off to the right, towards Telouet. About 6 km before the village, there are several areas of flat red earth and spiky grass that are good for camping.

Telouet

Although the region is apparently deserted, campers are unlikely to find themselves alone for long. Young men, on donkeys or on foot, will gather at a discreet distance from your tents, to spend hours gazing at the routine of campsite life. A more unfriendly guest is the scorpion, which can often be found beneath nearby boulders. Despite the lack of water in the area, dragonflies (the powder post blue darter, for example) are especially common. During the summer, nearby rivers are dry, with white incrustations of salt. An amazing range of rocks and minerals add colour to the surrounding mountainsides.

The village of Telouet, High Atlas, viewed from the kasbah

The village of Telouet, as with so many of the settlements of the Atlas, blends into the earthy colours of the mountainous landscape around it. Other than a café, there is little to see here. Thursday's vegetable market is worth a look – traders bring their produce along the twisting road from dawn onwards. The main attraction, however, is undoubtedly the wonderful kasbah complex of the Glaoui brothers.

Madani and T'Hami rose from the ranks of the other Berber chieftains towards the end of the last century. They had the good sense to offer lavish hospitality to Sultan Moulay Hassan, on an occasion when he was returning from a military expedition to the Tafilalt, during a particularly harsh winter. In return, the sultan gave them control over vast tracts of land in southern Morocco, and also provided them with weapons left over from the Tafilalt campaign. When the French arrived, twenty years later, they were content to leave the Glaoui in effective control.

The kasbah of Telouet was the Glaoui brothers' headquarters. It stands on an area of flat ground to the south of the Telouet Pass. The road comes to an end beneath a high wall, topped with battlements and a minaret. Vehicles can be left here, while you make your way into the courtyard. This dusty space is strewn with fragments of wall, ironwork and other rubble. It is here that you are likely to meet the guardian. It is only sensible to accept his offer to show you around – not because his description is terribly helpful (especially if you cannot speak French), but because there are several dangerous areas where the fabric of the building has decayed. (The guardian sometimes trawls for prospective clients in the café in Telouet.)

Much of the kasbah has been destroyed or seriously damaged by flooding. Nonetheless, it is still worth a couple of hours' exploration. Its large cool rooms are superbly decorated. The relatively simple tiled pattern of the floor contrasts with the astounding intricacy of the walls – a multicoloured display of flowers, swirls and geometric shapes. The same motifs recur on the carved wooden doors. Perhaps most impressive, though, is the stuccoed plasterwork. In the short passageways and arches, the effect is like a three-dimensional cross-section of a honeycomb. The sections connecting the round columns to the ceilings are wonderfully detailed. Similarly, the large windows are partly covered by finely crafted ironwork. The effect of looking through these at the brown, baking village beyond is almost unreal.

This kasbah has been uninhabited by humans for many years now. The only residents now appear to be the bats, who huddle in black amorphous blobs, easily distinguishable against the bright colours of the ceilings. By climbing up on to an area of flat roof, you can see the many storks' nests that seem perilously unstable on the top of the towers and minarets. The birds seem to be holding their wings outstretched, as if afraid that they and their homes are in imminent danger of toppling to the ground. Looking from this terrace, past the battlements topped with square-base pyramids, you can gaze over the scenery of the High Atlas.

The descent to Marrakech

Back to the P31, turn right for the final 7 km drive up to the highest point of this crossing – the Tizi-n-Tichka Pass (2260 m). In fact, this is the highest roadway pass in the country. The mountains of Jbel Tistout (to the north-east) and Jbel Bou Ourioul (to the west) dominate the view.

Sixteen kilometres down from the pass, via a succession of unmissable photostops, is the village of Taddert. Perched on hillside terraces, amongst walnut trees, this is a delightful town situated in attractive countryside. After a brief climb to the pass of Tizi-n-Ait-Imguer, the remainder of the journey to Marrakech is all downhill. The vistas over the various valleys display an incredible blend of reds, browns, greens and greys.

Approaching Marrakech, the P31 passes through almond and olive groves, to a relatively cultivated plain. Vast piles of prickly pears can be seen at the roadside. Do not attempt to pick these yourself, as the thin spines are very painful and difficult to remove. You may well see children harvesting the pears – they use long pieces of split cane to dislodge the fruit from the thick, succulent plants.

Marrakech

The city

Marrakech was founded in the middle of the eleventh century, by Youssef ben Tachfin. It dominates the approaches to the strategically crucial High Atlas passes and the desert beyond. The Almoravids, of whom Youssef was the first leader, were replaced by the Almohads less than a hundred years later, as the ruling dynasty. Their empire stretched across north Africa and into Spain. Marrakech was developed to be its capital. By the middle of the thirteenth century, however, the influence of the city had waned.

Its fortunes rose and fell several times in the succeeding years. During the 'reign' of T'Hami el Glaoui, and since Moroccan independence from France, Marrakech has steadily grown in importance. Relatively efficient agriculture, together with a growth of industry and tourism, have combined to transform Marrakech into Morocco's second largest city (after Casablanca), with a population rising towards 700,000.

As with Fes, we shall not attempt to provide an exhaustive guide to the city, as the standard guide-books do this quite adequately. Instead, we aim to give a brief taste of this wonderful imperial centre, suggesting a few sights for the visitor with little time to spare. Above all, we would hope to convince even the most hardened countryside-chauvinist to devote a good while to this uniquely compelling city.

Arriving from the Tizi-n-Tichka Pass, the P31 curves up to the north of Marrakech, joining the P24 from Fes. Coming into the city, you will find yourself on the Avenue des Nations Unies, which runs parallel to the red mud and lime walls of the medina. The avenue leads to the Place du 16 Novembre, which you should cross straightover, leaving by the Avenue Hassan II. Take the third turning on the left – the broad Avenue de France. A short distance down the avenue, on the right-hand side, you will come to the camping site.

Again, as with Fes, it is probably sensible for reasonably large groups of campers to make use of the official site. You can be assured of a measure of security, as well as avoiding a considerable journey to the city centre. Even so, this campsite is about 40 minutes' walk from the centre of the medina. Vehicles can be left with guardians in the main square – the Djemaa El Fna. Obviously, if money and numbers allow, it is far more convenient to base yourself at cheap hotels in the medina. (These tend to cluster along the streets to the south of the Djemaa El Fna.)

In itself, the shady campsite is quite adequate. A small café sells soft drinks and postcards. There is even a swimming pool, although on our last visit anyone daring to use it would have had to share the water with a dead rat. A standpipe provides water for washing clothes and dishes.

The campsite stands on the south-western corner of Gueliz – the new town. Whole streets are lined by orange trees and lavender-blue riots of jacaranda. Built by the French, it is almost without any redeeming features of interest. There are few facilities here that are not available in the medina as well. Walking from the site, turn right along the Avenue de France, and then left along the Rue Moulay el Hassan. This leads straight up to the Place de la Liberté, which stands opposite a kink in the medina walls. On the other side of the Place, and to the left, is the Bab Nkob, from where the Avenue Mohammed V leads into the old town.

As you walk along the avenue, the minaret of the Koutoubia Mosque gradually looms larger. Seventy-one metres in height, and 13 m wide, the tower of 'the bookseller's mosque' is the focal point of the Marrakech skyline. Built in the final years of the twelfth century, it has now lost the coloured plasterwork that once covered it, although part of a mosaic of blue ceramic tiles remains on the upper part of the tower. You can gain some idea of the original decoration by visiting the fully restored Mosque of the Kasbah, which lies some way to the south. Note that the carved patterns differ on each of the minaret's four faces. Look out for the three gold-coloured balls on top.

As you come to the Koutoubia, turn left and you will soon arrive in the large open space that is the heart of Marrakech's medina. The translation of 'Djemaa el Fna' is far from certain. It is generally taken to mean 'Place of the Dead'. This grisly title is justified by the square's early role as a place of execution, where the severed heads of malefactors were displayed as a gory deterrent.

The medina at Marrakech

The best time at which to visit the Djemaa is during late afternoon or the evening. Bustling with people, it is like a vast fairground. Wandering through the milling crowds, you can stop to watch rubber-limbed acrobats, dancers, actors, musicians and storytellers. Animals play an important part in the entertainment; elderly men lift tambourines revealing drugged snakes that are coaxed into activity, moth-eaten monkeys are urged to display their acrobatic talents, while large, long-tongued lizards just sit and, well, sit!

Various sales pitches are also spread out in the square, often under the shade of umbrellas. Young boys sell slabs of gooey sweetmeats from trays, while numerous children rush up to you, persistently demanding that you buy their jewellery or cedarwood-handled kebab skewers. Perhaps the most avoidable stalls in the Djemaa are those of the tooth-pullers, where recently uprooted, decayed molars are displayed on a small piece of cloth. The most colourful figures are the water-sellers. They are brightly clothed and announce their presence with a tinkling bell, as they offer a cup of water from their polished brass vessels.

During the evening, be sure to wander around the enormous array of food stalls that cluster to one side of the square. Customers sit at a low bench, faced with a dazzling variety of bowls of food. Couscous, salads, vegetables, rice, chicken, tomatoes, stews, fish, snails and kebabs can all be sampled for very little expense. With discretion the better part of intestinal valour, it is probably advisable to confine yourself to viewing the food at the open-air stalls, eating in the relative safety of one of the cheap restaurants around the Djemaa. Alternatively, try the truffles, aphrodisiac tea or fresh orange juice that are dispensed from smaller stalls in the quieter reaches of the square. At night, you may want to spend a little more by finding a café with a terrace overlooking the square below.

Visitors to Marrakech's medina must be prepared for the non-stop stream of hustlers, hideously deformed beggars, drug peddlars and potential guides who plague any Europeans that appear. As always, the best strategy is to be firm but polite with any whose attentions you wish to avoid. They are remarkably insistent, but get the message eventually. Serious trouble is most unlikely. It is a good idea to use a money-belt in the medina, as the bustling crowds are an ideal environment for pickpockets.

Once soaked in the atmosphere of the Djemaa el Fna, make your way north into the network of souks. Relatively fragrant in comparison to Fes, you find that the danger is no longer in being barged by an overloaded donkey, but in being harassed by an impatient youth on a moped. Navigation through the narrow, covered streets is naturally difficult. Standard guide-books usually contain maps of the souks. Alternatively, you can employ a guide to show you through (although the same warnings apply as in Fes). Having said this, we have found that the best approach is simply to wander where the spirit leads, at least if you are not alone. If necessary, you can always pay a small child to lead you back to the Djemaa.

A wide range of goods are available, from obvious tourist tat to some wonderful bargains. Carpets, rugs, metalwork and clothing are much in evidence. More interesting, though, are the wooden items (often marquetry made on the coast and bought in), the leatherwork and the spices. Some of the spice shops provide a range of ingredients for magic spells – dried chameleons, dead owls and jackals' feet, for example. It is also well worth wandering into a spice shop, just to marvel at the range of variously coloured curiosities, and to inhale the gorgeously pungent bouquet. A request for mint tea, or the roots from which the aphrodisiac tea sold in the Djemaa are made, can often result in a couple of hours chatting and sampling in one of these tiny emporia. You will find it hard to miss the shops selling 'babouches'. These soft leather, heelless slippers are stacked by the thousand – surrounding their eager purveyor.

If time permits, try to walk south from the souks and the Djemaa, to the Saadian tombs. Leave the square by the Rue Bab Agnaou. At its end you reach a square by two city gates. Go through the left-hand one and you will soon reach the Mosque of the Kasbah. A small passageway runs along the right-hand side of the mosque, leading into an enclosure. High walls encompass a selection of superbly overdecorated mausoleums and smaller burial monuments. This is a delightful spot in which to spend some time away from the city's frenetic activity. Most of the tombs date from the sixteenth, seventeenth and eighteenth centuries.

The ideal conclusion to a night in the medina is to return to the campsite in a 'caleche'. These horse-drawn buggies are relatively cheap if you muster together a party of five, and they are certainly the most atmospheric way to travel through the warm summer nights.

The Atlantic Coast

Essaouira

The Dunes of Cap Sim

The journey west from Marrakech to the Atlantic is singularly unexciting. Route P10 leads 150 km across a plain that is almost entirely without interest. Once you pass the village of Sidi Moktar, keep an eye open for argan trees. These trees have a very limited distribution, and this is one of the few remaining localities in which they can be found. Goats are able to climb up into the branches to feed. This is leading to the demise of the argan. The nuts picked from these plants are used to provide oil.

Rather than heading straight into Essaouria, you should cut south on the P8, just past Ounara. As you do so, it is possible to catch a glimpse of the sea and the twin Purpuraires Islands, beyond the gleaming white buildings of the town. In Roman times, these islands were the site of dye-working centres, established by a local Berber prince. Thirty kilometres later, a signpost indicates a track to Sidi Kaouki, on the right-hand side of the P8. The track

An example of the argan tree, now dying out due to goats feeding in the branches

leads over rough ground to a long beach. A hundred metres or so back from the Atlantic rollers, there are areas of flat ground next to a shallow lake. These are ideal for camping, although careful driving is required to avoid unobvious patches of soft, wet sand. The only other real hazard for campers is the occasional blast of wind off the sea, which can whip up sand and search out any weaknesses in tent erection technique. If the wind is particularly problematic, there are patches of tamarisk near the lake and large rocky outcrops a little way along the beach, which would both provide shelter.

This part of the coastline is an ideal location in which to stay, both as a base for exploring the seashore area itself, and for visiting Essaouira town. Although the beach is wonderfully unspoilt for bathing, beware of the power of the long-shore currents which can be very dangerous.

A spare morning would be well spent climbing up and inland from the beach. The lake is home to terrapins and frogs, while tortoises can be found in the sand dunes. Although tortoises tend to be inactive during the summer heat, it is not unusual to see them on the cooler dunes. Wading birds frequent the lake and a number of species fly up and down the coast. The large black birds are southern cormorants, distinguished by white feathers around the head. A couple of kilometres up and in from the shore, you will find a delightful village of blindingly white Berber houses. It is far from impossible that a curious farmer here will invite you in to meet his family, and enjoy a meal of biscuits, fruit and mint tea.

The town of 'Mogador'

The port of Mogador, now known as Essaouira, is a delightful contrast to the sweltering bustle of inland Marrakech. Although pirates had settled in the area earlier, the town was established in the middle of the eighteenth century, to a French design. Approaching the town, you join the Boulevard Mohammed V, which runs parallel to the long sandy beach. Leave your vehicles in the spaces near the walls of the old city. Before entering the medina itself, look out at the dramatic fortifications of the harbour. The 'skala' stands silhouetted against the sea – a gun platform topped by a series of cannon once used to defend this flourishing trading centre.

Enter the medina through the Bab Sebaa, which lies at the end of the Boulevard. The vast, studded, wooden gate is set in a stone arch, which itself contrasts with the scruffy brown/red walls of the

The Portugese town of Essaouira

medina. Once inside, there are few specific things that you should aim to see. Nonetheless, there are few more pleasant spots in Morocco to enjoy a morning's aimless wandering. Do make sure, though, that you walk through to the far side of the medina, to the woodworkers' souk. Many of the items of marquetry on view in the shops of Marrakech were originally crafted in the dark workshops which lurk off these narrow streets. As there is a largely assured 'export' market, the marked prices of the various items tend to be as good as fixed. Despite this, there are some really beautiful souvenirs to be bought here, at prices far lower than they would be in Europe. Thuya and cedarwood are the predominant materials used. The former is a dark wood, with an attractive, swirly grain. Letter-racks, cigar boxes, bowls, jewellery boxes and chess sets are all common. Some of the tables made here are quite exquisite. They are, however, expensive, as well as being somewhat awkward to fit in a backpack!

From the woodworkers' souk, you can follow the city walls to the left, leading out to the harbour. As well as scrambling over the windswept fortifications, take time to sample the delicious fresh sardines that are grilled over charcoal at stalls on the waterside. The regular restaurants in town also tend to specialise in seafood, and are generally of good quality. (For a between-meals nibble, keep an eye open for stalls selling peanuts toasted in brown sugar – alarmingly irresistible.)

If you have a vehicle, it is certainly well worth camping on the coast near Cap Sim, rather than in the town. The main campsite, a few hundred metres along the Boulevard Mohammed V on the seafront, should be avoided.

The Journey North

Introduction

Although it accounts for a distance of over 700 km, we will be making an intentionally brief description of the journey from Essaouira to Tangier, and of the sites en route. The main attractions of this coastal section are the large cities of Casablanca and Rabat/Sale. These are dealt with in depth by standard guide books. Furthermore, visitors concentrating on the natural history of Morocco, and thus having a limited time to spend in the main settlements, would (in our opinion) be well advised to concentrate on the less 'Western' cities of Fes and Marrakech. The traffic along the northern route is much more dense. When travelling around dusk, care should be taken, as unlit tractors, carts and animals are frequently on the road.

Essaouira to El-Jadida

As you leave Essaouira, join the P10, which cuts 24 km east to Ounara. From there, it is just under 100 km to Tleta-de-Sidi-Bouguedra, on the P8. The town of Safi lies 26 km west, along the P12. Of Portuguese origin, this is now an unattractive fishing port and industrial centre. The medina contains little of note, with the possible exception of a potteries quarter. There is an official campsite a couple of kilometres to the north of the town, near the (dirty) beach of Sidi Bouzid.

Leaving Tleta-de-Sidi-Bouguedra, the P8 reaches the coast again within 70 km, at the town of El-Jadida. This is a quick journey, although the S121, which hugs the coast, is certainly a more attractive option.

In common with Safi, the first serious development here was undertaken by the Portuguese. The beach is popular with Moroccan holidaymakers, so consequently accommodation can be scarce in the summer months. If you have an hour or so to spend in El-

Jadida, walk down the main street. Halfway along, a small entrance leads off to the Portuguese cistern. Water covers the paving stones of a sixteenth century vaulted chamber, originally built as a precaution in the event of a siege.

Casablanca and Rabat

Casablanca lies 81 km along the P8 from the El-Jadida junction. This is Morocco's largest and most important city. Its growing dominance stems from the arrival of the French early this century. It remains as much European as Moroccan. Any comprehensive guide to Morocco will describe the city, although you need have few qualms about missing it altogether.

Departing from Casablanca, on the 90 km journey to Rabat, you are faced with the choice of a motorway, the coast road, or the P1 (which has a speed limit of 60 mph).

Rabat is the Moroccan centre of government. It lacks the lively spirit of Marrakech or Fes, but at least is not devoid of architectural interest, an accusation which could not unfairly be levelled at Casablanca. It lies on the southern bank of the Oued Bou Regreg (the 'Father of Reflections'), with the medina of Sale (the older of the two towns) to the north. Given the choice, Rabat and Sale undoubtedly merit more attention than their larger neighbour, 90 km down the coast.

Rabat to Tangier

Heading north from Sale, the P2 reaches the industrial town and port of Kenitra in 40 km. For the next 80 km, the road roughly follows the course of the Oued Sebou, to Souk-el-Arba-du-Rharb. This is a fertile region. Its vulnerability to periodic flooding has now been ameliorated by judicious damming. Ksar-el-Kebir 40 km north, has an interesting medina. The next 40 km stretch of the P2 skirts the edge of the fertile plain of the Oued Loukos, as both road and river make their way through salt marshes to the coast at Larache, yet another fishing port. If you have time to spare here, it is better spent in Lixus, a couple of kilometres to the north, than in Larache itself.

Lixus is the site of a Roman town. Visible ruins include various temples and a set of baths, which contain an impressive mosaic of the head of Poseidon. There is a theatre on the high ground.

Crossing an area of hills, you are left with a further 70 km, before reaching Tangier. Several roadside stalls offer a chance to stock up on melons. After hugging the golden, sandy coast for 25 km or so, the P2 cuts inland from the airport, finally entering Tangier through its dingy, run-down suburbs, complete with shabby tower blocks.

Tangier

Tangier is a city with ancient origins, supposedly founded by Antea, the giant son of Neptune. More certain, though, is the importance of the port (then called Tingis) to the Phoenicians and the Greeks as a trading centre. After a period as the capital of the Roman province of Mauritania, the Vandals occupied the city until the close of the fifth century. Under the control of Arab dynasties until seized by Portugal in the 1470's, Tangier then entered a period during which it was subject to continued rivalry among European nations and native rulers. Relative political stability in the twentieth century brought an important international role, which in turn enabled the city to flourish. Unfortunately, Tangier has suffered relative decline since its incorporation into the independent Kingdom of Morocco, as its special international status has disappeared.

Completing a circuit of Morocco, you may well feel the need for a couple of days' rest and recuperation before heading back to Europe. If so, Tangier is an attractive and friendly place in which to spend them. The historical and present-day importance of foreign visitors gives a wholly different feel to the town, in comparison with the imperial capitals inland. In addition,we found Tangier to have a more compelling atmosphere than the large west-coast ports.

Accommodating large groups here in the summer is not a cheap business. Your best bet is the Camping Miramonte, a couple of kilometres to the west of the town centre. Not too expensive, it can be fairly crowded in the summer. More pricey, about 5 km to the west of the town, is Camping Tingis. The facilities are better here, though, and it is convenient for the beach of the Bay of Tangier.

During the evening, walk along the palm-lined Avenue d'Espagne, which follows the line of the beach. It is edged by numerous cafés, ice-cream parlours and restaurants, all of which are lively places in which to spend part of the evening. At the end of the beach, the sand gives way to the first arm of the port. Continue along the avenue until you reach the corner of the medina. The Place de la Tannerie stands here, at a gap in the old walls. Walk through the gap, and up the steep steps of the Rue de la Tannerie, to Moulay Ismail's Grand Mosque. Access, as always in Morocco, is forbidden to infidels, so turn left along the Rue de la Poste, which takes you to the Petit Socco. (If you are on your own at night, you may prefer to take the longer route, via the Grand Socco.) The Petit Socco, which used to be a cosmopolitan meeting-place for traders from various countries, is now a small, café-lined square. From here, the tourist-oriented Rue es Siaghin runs to the other side of the medina, and the Grand Socco. The Grand Socco is a large square just outside the medina walls. Like many such places in north Africa, its original market function has been largely supplanted by the requirements of the bus company! Nonetheless it is still a lively spot, and some of its cafés are quite pleasant. The market itself now takes place in the streets and alleys around the Grand Socco on Thursdays and Sundays.

The high ground of the medina offers some superb views over the port, the Bay of Tangier and the Straits of Gibraltar. Make your way up from the Petit Socco, via the Rue des Chretiens and the Rue Ben Raisouli, to the Bab el Assa and the Place de la Kasbah.

Leaving Tangier by ferry for Algeciras, you will have to make your way to the western of the two arms of the port. Do not approach this crossing without a suitably laid-back attitude. You will have to arrive 60 minutes before your official departure time. Obtain your embarkation card from the ferry company desk and have your passport stamped before you make your way through to customs. Dealing with officialdom at this port would try the patience of a saint. Console yourself with the thought that within a couple of hours, you will be relaxing on the deck, gazing at the spectacular profile of Gibraltar slipping by.

ALGERIA

A tamarisk bush and camel in the Grand Erg Occidental

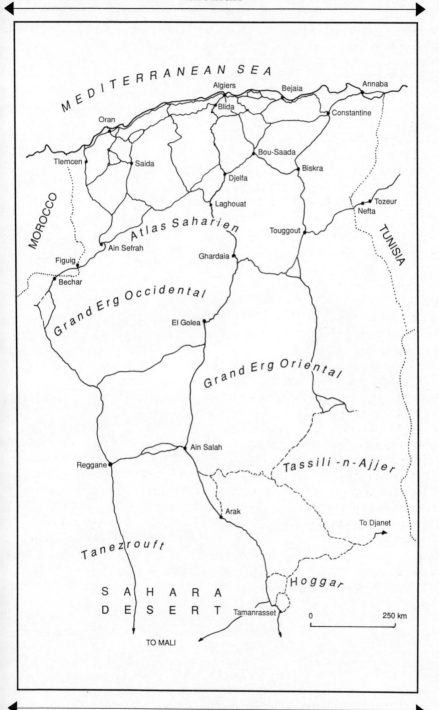

Introduction

Algeria is the third largest country in Africa. Its 2¹/₂ million kilometres constitute an area five times that of Morocco, although their populations are roughly the same.

The Algerian Atlas range is lower than the mountain peaks of Morocco. The highest point is Mount Tahat (in the Hoggar Mountains) at over 2,900 m. The Hoggar are found in the south of the country. To the north-east lie the Tassili. This range is famous for the wealth of cave paintings that have been preserved by its arid climate.

Against a magnificent backdrop of classic sand dune desert, Algeria offers the remnants of Roman occupation to explore, as well as a diverse cultural tapestry. After a single visit, many people find that Algeria continues to haunt them, and they are compelled to return.

In terms of tourism, Algeria is without doubt the least developed of the three countries that we consider in this book. Consequently, many of the trappings that tourism brings to the visitor, such as the attentions of hordes of small children, are largely absent.

Geography

Bordered by the Mediterranean in the north, Algeria stretches for over 1,500 km, to Niger in the south. This distance encompasses a number of geographical regions. Along the coast are the highlands of the Atlas Tellien, a continuation of the fold mountains of the Moroccan Atlas. Driving south from Algiers, the chain is 130 km wide. To the east, where it incorporates the Massif de l'Aures, the width increases to more than 200 km. This is a beautiful region of high mountain passes and steep canyons. The coastal scenery is spectacular, with its high cliffs and winding roads. Villages and towns tend to be fairly isolated in this high country. On their southern edge the mountains give way to a plateau that extends from Tunisia to Morocco. The characteristic feature of this region is the presence of salt lakes which dry up in summer. These are called 'chotts'. Chott Ech Chergui is inland from Oran and stretches over 150 km in length.

A narrow strip of mountains, the Saharan Atlas, separates the Chotts from the Sahara Desert. The desert here is erg – great seas of shifting sand. To the west lies the Grand Erg Occidental and to the east, the Grand Erg Oriental. A tarmac road runs between them, connecting northern and southern Algeria. It is almost impossible to cross the ergs themselves by normal means. There is no road or supply of water, and the entire area consists of mobile dune. Few living things are able to survive. Any vegetation that might try to develop is soon engulfed by the shifting sand.

This central region of Algeria is a stony desert plateau, running towards the Hoggar Mountains. These rise to over 2,500 m in height and are an impressive set of 'volcanic plugs'. (A volcanic plug consists of the solidified lava that once filled the central chamber of a volcano. It is left behind as the softer surrounding rock erodes away. Eroded debris remains around the base of the plug.)

North-east of the Hoggar is another and more remote range – that of Tassili-n-Ajjer. This was one of the homes of neolithic man. The area contains some of the best preserved cave paintings in the world. Many depict the animals that were hunted here before the area became desertified. There is a great deal of water here, contained in tiny hollows. You can also see ancient trees that are believed to be thousands of years old.

Climate

The climate varies across the different regions of Algeria, as well as with altitude. Snow is common in the Atlas during winter, blocking many mountain passes. Even the Hoggar may have snow for part of the year. Summer temperatures are high throughout the country. Daily maximum values are consistently over 40°C (104°F). At night the temperature may drop somewhat, but even so, it can only be considered cold in the winter or at high altitudes. On high ground you may be troubled by strong winds in the late afternoon.

In desert areas there is always the possibility of sand storms. True sand and dust storms are the result of a sudden fall in the air's moisture content. The change in pressure can raise a cloud of sand hundreds of metres in height. If you are caught in such a cloud, visibility is completely obscured.

Driving in Algeria

In the north the main roads are metalled and should present few problems. Along the coastal fringe there are numerous hairpin bends and few signs. As you move towards the desert, so the roads deteriorate. For some years the main road from Algeria to Tamanrasset – in the centre of the desert – has been metalled. This is the central artery of communication to southern Algeria. Consequently, it bears the heaviest traffic of the southward routes. This means that you may see up to half a dozen vehicles in any one hour. Other roads to the south boast only one vehicle a week. The traffic is not the result of tourism. It largely consists of the heavy trucks that supply the southern Algerian towns. These giant, air-conditioned Volvo and Mercedes juggernauts operate in small convoys. Huge fat tyres provide flotation on the sand. Over the years these have caused the partial break-up of the Tamanrasset road. Large potholes appear at regular intervals. It is often wise to drive on the sand or stones that fringe the road. Hitting a pothole or the side of the road at speed virtually guarantees a burst tyre, especially if you use sand tyres. Road maintenance in the desert is undertaken by Algerian army conscripts. The quality is fairly poor.

Apart from the Tamanrasset route, roads are of a very poor quality away from the towns. The surface is generally either sand or stones. Remember that even tarmac roads develop corrugations. These can mean a very bumpy ride.

Petrol and diesel can usually be obtained without difficulty in the towns. The latter is very cheap. Towns (and hence sources of fuel) are few and far between in the Sahara. This increases the importance of forward planning. Vehicle spares are virtually non-existent outside the major cities. You should carry your own spares – see the list in 'Planning and Preparation', p.37.

On entering the country you will be required to show your Carnet de Passage (unnecessary in Morocco or Tunisia). You should obtain this from one of the motoring organisations before you leave the UK. It costs approximately £30. You will also have to buy vehicle insurance when you reach the border.

Maps

The Michelin 153 is still the best general map of the entire country. Detailed maps of certain parts of the desert have been prepared from Landsat satellite photographs. Unfortunately, as the geography of the desert is constantly changing, the detail is often inaccurate.

Currency and Bureaucracy

The Algerian dinar is divided into 100 centimes.

Dinars must be obtained within Algeria itself. All the main banks can be found in Algiers and the other important cities and towns. Away from these it is difficult to exchange currency. Credit cards are of limited use, even in Algiers and Oran. You will probably find it difficult to use local currency to pay bills in the large hotels or to pay for flights. It is therefore sensible to carry dollars or sterling in addition to dinars.

Several bureaucratic procedures must be endured when you enter Algeria. As we noted above, you will need a Carnet de Passage if you are bringing a vehicle.

More irritating, however, is the requirement that each visitor to Algeria must spend at least £150 during their stay. Consequently, you must keep the receipts whenever you change money, and show these to officials when you leave. For individuals or small groups this may present few problems, especially if you stay in hotels. Students and larger groups who are camping, however, may have problems spending as much as this. Algeria, unlike Morocco and Tunisia, is not developed in tourist terms and therefore has few souvenirs for sale, so that option is little use. Do not forget that if you are travelling through Algeria, to Niger or Mali for example, with the intention of returning via Algeria, you will be required to spend this amount twice.

Customs and other officials in Algeria are normally helpful and friendly. Entering and leaving the country should present fewer difficulties than in Morocco.

Language

Despite the range of dialects spoken in Algeria, most people will be able to communicate in French.

Camping and Accommodation

Campsites are found in the larger towns and are usually quite reasonable, both in terms of cost and facilities. Outside these the opportunities are endless.

The harvesting of crops takes place in May and June. By midsummer there is little sign of agriculture, and the ground becomes baked hard. Erecting tents can thus be difficult, and you will have to use as few pegs as possible. However, camping without tents is common practice, especially in the desert.

Reasonable accommodation can be found for less than £2 per night. It is important to realise that the 'travellers' season' in Algeria lies outside the summer months. Hence, if you arrive at the campsite in Tamanrasset in July you will find it almost empty, whereas it will be almost full in the months of early spring.

Food and Water

The price of food varies from expensive to astronomical. You will invariably pay three or more times as much as you would in Morocco. In addition, the price rises as you move south. In many areas the range of food available is very limited. In the Saharan region it may only be possible to find melons, dates and a few vegetables (such as onions and pumpkins). Supplies are always plentiful, but expensive. A melon may cost more than £5. As in other north African countries, the main market is the place to buy food.

Cakes and bread are more reasonably priced. They can easily be obtained in the towns. Vineyards are common in the north and wine is therefore widely available.

Supplies of water can obviously be a problem. It is available from taps in the towns. Sources of *eau potable* are clearly marked on the Michelin 153 map.

Algiers

The City

Our starting point is Algiers – location of the main docks and international airports. Arriving with a vehicle, you will probably have fewer problems with the dock officials than you would in most other countries of north Africa. Nonetheless, you should still allow several hours for the necessary form filling. If you come off a ferry without a vehicle, you will find the train and bus station towards the north of the dock. In the far north of the quay area there is a fascinating fish market – close to the Great Mosque! The main road along the seafront here is the Boulevard de Che Guevara. Just west of the fish market the boulevard ends in the Martyrs' Square. This is a good central base from which to walk in search of Algiers' more interesting sights.

This picturesque part of the city is given colour by its palms and flowers. The buildings are large and imposing. Some are impressive examples of modern architecture. The National Assembly stands at the junction of the Boulevard de Che Guevara and the Boulevard Zighout Youcef. Beyond it is the City Hall. The railway station can be found nearby, as can the Government Palace in the Esplanade de l'Afrique. Many of the boulevards are given a colonial feel by their colonnades and whitewashed walls.

From the Martyrs' Square, it is just a short walk to the Kasbah. A maze of tiny streets seem to radiate from the square and across the hills. Between the square and the Kasbah, there are several interesting mosques. In addition, look out for the Palace of the Princesses – the sixteenth century Dar Azizia. The fort stands near the highest point of the Kasbah. Given its ruined state, its most useful function is to serve as a landmark, offering some guidance as you make your way through the run-down, but distinctive, streets of the Kasbah. Guides – both official and unofficial – will press their services upon you. They are far from essential, however, especially as the Kasbah is on a slope. If you become lost, simply make your way down the hill to the Rue Amar Ali.

In the southern part of the city there is a pleasant botanical garden and small zoo. Opposite these are the Pasteur Institute and the Museum of Fine Arts. One museum well worth visiting is the Villa du Bardo at the end of Rue Didouche Mourad. Collections of ancient rock art are kept within the rooms of the villa. These include cave paintings from Tassili and other regions of Algeria. There is also a display of the remains of prehistoric animals and humans, taken from the Sahara.

The area around the Villa du Bardo offers a glimpse of an unfamiliarly affluent Algeria. The university, an ornate post office, tourist shops and the official Algerian Handicraft centre are all nearby. In the last of these, fixed prices are charged, so you can avoid haggling.

As you leave the heart of Algiers, you move into a typically dismal and decayed north African suburban sprawl.

The Environs

In years gone by, the Barbary Coast was infamous for its roving pirates, who plundered Mediterranean shipping. Today the pirates are gone, but the coast remains a delightful and often spectacular region to visit. Where the Atlas ranges meet the sea, steep cliffs and rugged coast merge with sandy bays. As the demands of tourism inexorably increase, more and more of these are being converted into 'resorts'. The 90 km of shoreline between Algiers and Cherchell (to the west) has become dominated by new resorts. Sidi Fredj is one of the better ones. Cherchell itself is the ancient Roman capital of Mauritania. There are numerous antiquities worth visiting. Along the N11 is Tipasa – overlooking the Mediterranean. The Roman remains to be found here include an amphitheatre.

Beyond Cherchell, the road to Oran is breathtaking. It passes through the Massif de Dahara, a magnificent series of forested mountains. The winding road clings to the rocky headlands, always providing an impressive view of this wild and desolate region. It is a good area for the birdwatcher, with a good chance of sighting peregrines and vultures. The botany is also fascinating because of the blend of European species (this being the fringe of their geographical range) and those of the northern Sahara. A particularly worthwhile stop for the naturalist is the estuary of the river Messelmoun, near Gouraya. When the current is flowing, water birds are numerous. In spring, a range of annual plants colonise the river sediments.

The coast to the east of Algiers is not as interesting. There is, however, an important National Park inland near Bouira. If you have time, this certainly merits a visit. Camping here is straightforward, with official sites provided. The area is set in the midst of the most impressive of Algeria's northern mountains, the Massif du Djurdjura. Heavily forested, it is almost as though they were a continuation of the Moroccan Middle Atlas. Snow or rockfalls mean that the tracks from Bouira may not always be open. It is therefore sensible to make enquiries in the town about routes and maps. The highest peaks are over 2,000 m in height. Several are used as ski resorts.

The Route to the Desert

Algiers to Ghardaia

En route to Blida, the main N1 road from Algiers passes through a fertile region of orange groves and vineyards – the Mitidja Plain. It is not long before you have passed through the bustling town of Blida, and the road begins to climb. The N1 follows a railway and the course of a river as it makes its way through the mountains, via the Chiffa Gorge. As in many other parts of the Atlas, the highlands here are cloaked in a forest of cedar – the ideal habitat for the Barbary ape. This species of macaque was once a common sight throughout these ranges. Sadly, the fragmentation of the forest has meant that the number of macaques has diminished along with the extent of their habitat. One of the few places in Algeria where they can now be seen is the Ruisseau des Singes, along the Chiffa Gorge. They spend their time begging food from tourists and travellers, like their relatives in Gibraltar.

The Chiffa Gorge is one of the most striking in Algeria. At its conclusion – the top of the pass at Col Ben Chikao (1,230 m) – the view is breathtaking. You soon reach the town of Medea – an Islamic holy place. It has often been referred to as the 'key to the south'. Once marauders or armies had passed through here, there was little to stop them before the Sahara. It is certainly true that, having passed through Medea, you are leaving the spectacle of mountains and gorges behind you.

Descending on to the mountain plateau, you pass through the small settlement of Ksar-el-Boukhari. This lies in the centre of a region of salt steppe. It is inhabited by Berber tribesmen, together with their goats and sheep. Further along the main road, there are two reservoirs fed by the Oued Nahar Ouassel. Beyond these the terrain is largely chott – salt lakes and salt pans. Much of the vegetation that is able to survive in this environment is halophytic, which is to say that it can tolerate the salt brought to the surface by the evaporation of soil water.

Far to the east lie mobile sand dunes which extend to Bou-Saada.

The railway from Algiers terminates at Djelfa, high up in the mountains of Ouled Nail. By road, the journey is about 400 km. Djelfa is a large oasis – the closest to Algiers (250 km). It lies on the road to Bou-Saada. There are a large number of shops here. They include the state-controlled craft stores, which sell silk, jewellry and camel-hair rugs at fixed prices. A textile factory in the town makes excellent djellabahs, which are available in the shops and from the market. (The market is also the place to find local wood carvings and metalwork.) Many of the textiles to be bought in the Bou-Saada region are in black and red, the traditional colours of the region.

From its beginnings as a small village, this town has grown considerably in recent years. Nonetheless, it is still an attractive place. Thousands of palm trees line the river, which flows beneath a steep rock face. There is an interesting walk upstream through the gorge of Gobr El Oucif – a round trip of 3–4 km. Bou-Saada itself is surrounded by spectacular mobile dunes.

Beyond Djelfa is Ain El Bell, with its collection of Roman ruins. The road along to Laghouat is a relatively uninteresting stretch. The town, though, is worth a stop. In the centre is the Grand Mosque. From its minaret, you can look over the avenues and palmeries of Laghouat itself, and over to the desert and mountains beyond. There are all the usual features of a typical desert town here, including the ubiquitous *piscine*.

Laghouat stands at the junction of a number of roads through the Saharan Atlas. An especially interesting detour heads west along their fringe. The route leads to Ain Sefra and eventually to the beautiful Bechar valley (dealt with at the end of this chapter). The roads are well-metalled and signposted. The main attraction is not the mountains, but the numerous cave paintings along the route. There are a few such sites just north of Laghouat, off the N47. One of the best is at Ain Sfisifs – just beyond the oasis of El Ghicha.

After following the N47 for about 30 km, take a turning on the left to Tadjmout which lies about 12 km away. A right turn in the village will put you on a track that leads to some rock paintings at Nambous. To reach Ain Sfisifs, however, you must continue through the village. After 20 km or so, take a right-hand track which eventually leads to the N47, just past Afflou. El Ghicha is 20 km further on. Here (and beyond the village by another 7 km) you will be able to see rock paintings. Near the village is a rock wall behind a derelict mill building. The paintings here show a whole series of different animals. Those further along the road at Ain Sfisifs depict elephants, snakes and lions. The terrain here is also attractive. The valley is cloaked with trees, including juniper and holm oak.

Heading south, you will see some of the numerous pipelines that trace their way across the landscape. This region of the northern Sahara is very rich in crude oil – especially near Ouargla, to the east of Ghardaia. The oil is pumped northwards to Oran, on the coast. The pipeline crosses the N1, just north of Ghardaia. This town is one of the most delightful places in the Sahara and well worth a stop.

Ghardaia to Ain Salah

Ghardaia is the largest town we have met so far on the N1, after Algiers. It even has its own international airport. Ghardaia has been the capital of the fertile M'Zab Valley since the 1050s. The

The tarmac road to Tamanrasset, near Ain Salah

valley's name is derived from the people who settled here in the eleventh century, dissatisfied with orthodox Islam – the Mozabites. These nomadic Berbers are unique in their philosophy and strict in their religious observance. The town has grown up as the coalescence of five villages lying in the gorge. These settlements are still fairly well defined. The most distinct is the Holy City of Beni Isguen – set behind walls that overlook the rest of Ghardaia. It is best to use an official guide to explore the Holy City. There are no tourist trappings, such as cafés or shops. Photography is banned. Not so long ago the gates of the city were locked at night. Even today, visitors are not welcome to stay overnight. When prayers are said, between midday and four in the afternoon, tourists are generally excluded from the city.

Other settlements to be found in this delightful oasis area include El Atteuff and Melika. From the latter there is a beautiful view of the rest of Ghardaia. The whitewashed houses have walls decorated with ochre figures. They are supplied with water that has been pumped to watertowers from thousands of deep wells. This is a truly delightful oasis to rest in and to wander through. The cemeteries of Melika and Ghardaia are well worth a visit to see the variety of monuments and architectural designs. The stagnant pool at El Atteuff is a haven for croaking frogs, toads and dragonflies. There is a wide range of hotels, as well as a guarded campsite.

If your route south started from Tunis, and you crossed the border from Tozeur and Nefta, then your journey links up with the N1 just to the south of Ghardaia. The road from Tunis is of good quality. It also offers a wonderful view of sand-dunes in the early stages around El Oued. These mobile sand-dunes occasionally create problems when they drift across the road.

Once you have left Ghardaia, the road climbs out of the shallow gorge and on to a stony plateau that continues for the 250 km to El Golea. The hamada (rock desert) landscape appears to be devoid of any wildlife. A few thorn bushes are all that seems to survive. It is not uncommon, however, to find a herd of gazelle here, and along the rest of this southward stretch to Tamanrasset.

El Golea is on the very edge of the Grand Erg Occidental – a vast expanse of Saharan dunes. Be sure to make an early start one morning, and climb up on to the dunes before dawn. The sight of the sun rising over the desert and the oasis town is unforgettable. El Golea is a very different town from Ghardaia. It is pleasantly situated within a forest of palms, pines and eucalyptus trees. There is a large airport on the outskirts.

The Grand Erg Occidental, west of El Golea

If you are unable to explore the dunes at El Golea, you will find a similar site 70 km to the south. This is an excellent place in which to camp. Possibly because this dune system is much smaller than the Grand Ergs, the animal life is slightly more obvious. Jerboas and darkling beetles can be seen late in the evening. You should also be able to spot the curious trails of sidewinder snakes in the sand. During the heat of the day, it is tempting to find shade under one of the few tamarisk bushes. Unfortunately, the sidewinders often have much the same idea!

As the road leaves the dunes and heads into the stony desert once again, you pass a road on the left which leads to a ruined fort at Chebaba. The quality of the 1,000 km of asphalt road that stretches south to Tamanrasset now begins to deteriorate. The combination of a poor base, and the consistent pounding of the trucks that supply southern Algeria, ensures that the road plays host to a regular series of deep potholes. By taking these at any speed, you risk serious damage to tyres and steering. Most people find it necessary to drive alongside the road. As the extent of the rutting increases, so the road/track spreads outwards. This can produce problems if you are camping. Get well clear of the road and sleep near your vehicle, as night traffic, which is very common, may not see you as it races across the sandy reg.

The N1 takes 400 km to cross the rocky Plateau du Tademait to Ain Salah. This desolate and rather boring journey is only enlivened by the still worsening potholes in the road. Arrival in the town of Ain Salah gives cause for excitement only because it marks the first change in scenery since El Golea. (There is one possible exception to this judgment: the point at which the road descends to Ain Salah from the high plateau. As it does so, the road winds through the Hadjadj Pass.)

Ain Salah to Reggane

If you have only limited time in Algeria, this is a suitable point at which to make the northward diversion to the Bechar valley. From Ain Salah, take the N52 to Reggane. The turning is signposted on the right. Two-wheel-drive vehicles will have to be handled with care over the scraped piste. About 50 km along this road from Ain Salah, there is a petrified forest. This is another sign of the life that once existed here before desertification took place. Sand storms are a common occurrence along this piste. The soft terrain necessitates low tyre pressures, in order to increase traction.

The main road near Arak

Aoulef lies 177 km from Ain Salah. This well-watered oasis is a real desert garden. Melons and tomatoes can be bought here, as well as a variety of other fruit and vegetables.

You will reach Reggane 130 km further on (see p.130).

Ain Salah to Tamanrasset

While in Ain Salah, it is only sensible to stock up with enough petrol/diesel to last until Tamanrasset, as fuel is not always available from the outposts of Arak and Ain Ecker. The asphalt road is very poor, with huge potholes. An otherwise monotonous journey is interspersed with a few diverting places en route. The Erg Mehedjibat is a small series of dunes to the west of the road. At Arak there is a gorge through the mountains. (It has to be admitted that this is not a particularly interesting gorge – but in comparison with the hundreds of kilometres preceding, it positively exudes excitement.) In addition, the road through the gorge is beautifully asphalted, with hardly a depression! This is due to the virtual impossibility of off-road driving in this area.

After a further 350 km, the southern settlement of Tamanrasset finally hoves into view.

Tamanrasset and the Hoggar Mountains

Tamanrasset

The city of Tamanrasset owes its importance to a military garrison that has been based here since the turn of the century. In recent years, this Tuareg stronghold has become better known as a stopping-off place for the increasing number of trans-Saharan expeditions. From here, there are piste connections on to Niger and Mali.

Set on the edge of the Hoggar Plateau, Tamanrasset is a well-known base from which to explore the mountains of the Hoggar. It is now possible to fly here. The resulting tourism has meant that the settlement is no longer the outpost that it once was. A number of hotels and a large campsite mean that there is a reasonable range of accommodation available. You may well find, however, that it is just as easy to camp outside the town, on the Hoggar route. The main advantage to be gained from staying in the town is the availability of water – better than outside, but still not certain. There are a few adequate shops, a market and even a tourist office.

Tamanrasset has grown considerably in recent years. It is now a rather sprawling place with high-rise apartments and a receiving station for satellite television. Parts of 'Tam' have a distinctly colonial feel to them. Tuaregs are a common sight – walking in the streets in their traditional robes.

Mechanics – together with spare parts – are in short supply here. Many of the parts which are available will be secondhand and suitable only for French cars.

Exploring the Hoggar

The Hoggar is one of the great natural wonders of the world. This high plateau – over 2,500 m high – is very desolate with no sign of any living creatures. The most striking feature of the Hoggar is the vast array of eroded volcanic plugs. Geological debris, from the erosion of the softer cones of the volcanoes, litters the region. There is an incredible stillness about these mountains, which seems to increase the atmosphere of desolation. Framed against a sunrise or sunset, the landscapes of the Hoggar are quite unforgettable.

There is a well-worn circular route from Tamanrasset. Take the track eastwards out of Tam, steadily climbing up into the Hoggar. After a short while, the winding road steepens considerably. Together with loose stones, this makes traction a problem. Land Rovers experience few difficulties, especially with low-range gears. Two-wheel-drive cars may face considerable problems. As the track curves back to Tam (after 100 km or so) it becomes quite dangerous.

Ninety kilometres from Tam, the track forks. The left fork stops at Assekrem, while the right fork starts the amazing trek to the eastern border with Libya.

Assekrem owes its fame (such as it is) to a hermit, Count Charles de Foucauld. During the nineteenth century this Frenchman was a great military strategist. He later became fascinated by the Arabs. Travelling widely in north Africa, he established a number of small monasteries, including one at Tamanrasset. In 1910 he built the hermitage at Assekrem, where he could meditate in the wilderness. Working as a Benedictine monk, he studied and wrote about the Tuaregs, who were being oppressed by the French at the time. Tragically, Charles was murdered there in 1916, by the very people

The Hoggar mountains

he was trying to help. The hermitage and chapel are still used by monks today. These followers of Foucauld are continuing his work with the Tuareg. The buildings are open to visitors, just a short climb up from the carpark.

The return journey brings you close to the spectacular peak of Iharen. This circular trek can easily be made in a day. If you have more time, though, spend the night near the hermitage and continue along the right fork – the Djanet route. This track goes through the Tin Teratimt Pass and is signposted to Hirafok. It is possible to camp there.

Staying on the Djanet track, make your way to Ideles, and then head south to Tahifet and on to Tam. This wider route takes in the sensational Azrou Pass, just before Tahifet. You can take a guide with you or contact the Algerian tourist office in Tam for an organised trek. Land Rovers and guides can be hired in the town.

While you are in Ideles, there is a fascinating detour northwards to Mertoutek. This is a good centre from which to explore the mountains (with a guide) in search of rock paintings and carvings. Most are relatively inaccessible by vehicle, so you will have to walk or take a donkey. This northern region of the Hoggar is excellent country for walking and climbing.

The magnificent spectacle of the volcanic plugs is well worth seeing. Unfortunately, the natural history is non-existent, barring the occasional acacia or thorn bush. During the night, it gets very cool and even by day warm clothing may be necessary. If you anticipate a long series of treks in the area, you would be well advised to employ a guide. They can not only show you the sights, but also help you locate the *gueltas*. These are small semi-permanent water holes that are found on the mountain sides.

The Road South to Niger

There is still 400 km of piste between Tamanrasset and the border with Niger to the south. This is a desolate desert, with no settlements. A crossing should only be attempted with considerable preparation and care. Once you leave the Hoggar plateau, the soft sand makes driving conditions very difficult.

West to Mali and the Tanezrouft

The Desert of Thirst

From Tamanrasset, the journey to Timeiaouine, on the Malian border, takes five or six days. The border crossing is fairly easy. You can then continue to Gao, or travel north, back into Algeria and on to Reggane. The latter route makes its way through the amazing but treacherous Tanezrouft, following the edge of the grand Erg Occidental. This northward trek brings you to the beautiful Bechar region – an area of classic oases that seem to have come straight from *Beau Geste*. This completes the circular tour of Algeria. If you do not have a four-wheel-drive vehicle, it is impossible to complete the journey up the western side of Algeria. Instead, you should take the N52 from Ain Salah to Reggane.

The route west from Tamanrasset should be tackled with a degree of trepidation. The piste varies from hard stony reg to very soft sand and mud. There are sources of petrol at various settlements en route. Unfortunately, this is no guarantee that fuel will actually be available at the time you pass through. Even if there are supplies on site, you will only be sold some if you are desperate, and you can prove it! Because of this, and the fact that such settlements are generally 400 km or so apart, you should aim to carry enough fuel for at least 1,500 km. Permission for making the journey should be obtained from the police in Tamanrasset. There is a Malian Consulate here which can issue visas. Bear in mind the consequences of making even the shortest visit to Mali. If you return to Algeria, you will again face the problem of having to spend £150 before you leave.

The naturalist will find this an interesting journey. The vegetation gradually changes as you progress from Tam to Mali. In spring, there can be a profusion of flowers in the area near Tit. Even in the summer months, bushes are a dominant feature. Near the border, the dominant vegetation becomes esparto grass and acacia. If you go as far as Gao, the river Niger supports a different range of wildlife.

Your first problem is to find the start of the track! Retrace your steps back along the N1 to Tit. This village was the scene of a battle

The river Niger, passing through Gao

between the Tuareg and French at the turn of the century. Just north of the village is the start of the piste. The entire route (including the point of departure) is marked by a series of stone cairns, called *balises*. These piles of stones are situated at intervals of 5 km. The early stage of the piste is badly corrugated. This has lead people to drive further and further away from the main track. After a while the route deviates considerably, according to which of the numerous tracks you follow. Fortunately, they all tend to go in the direction of Abelessa, 100 km from Tam. Abelessa is an amalgamation of several small villages. There is a set of rock paintings nearby, as well as the ruins of a Roman fort. This is believed to be the most southerly point that the Romans reached.

The track continues on the corrugated piste to Silet. Just north of here, there is a hilly area which includes an extinct volcano. As you leave Silet, the terrain deteriorates and navigation becomes more difficult. (This is the stretch of the Paris–Dakar rally in which Mark Thatcher got lost.) There are two passable tracks leaving Silet. The one to the south of the village goes to Fort Bordes (Tin Zaoaten) on the Malian border, and then eventually into the Adrar mountains. This is dangerous, and not recommended. If you decide to attempt the route, the police in Abelessa will be able to give information on the condition of the piste. The north-western track from Silet is slightly easier, but you should be prepared to dig out vehicles that have become bogged down.

A short distance from Silet, the road passes through Adrar Isket. Then after a stretch of sand, you move into a hilly region that serves to break the monotony of the landscape. One of the *balises* carries a sign to Tim Missaou – less than 10 km away. There is a well here, and a few kilometres further on there are several sets of rock paintings. Some of these were discovered by Henri Lhote, a famous Saharan explorer of the 1950s. A number of paintings show horses drawing what appear to be chariots. This led Lhote to support the theory that a chariot route from Rome to Gao (or even Timbuktu) once crossed the Sahara near here.

The last stop before Mali is the one-horse town of Timeiaouine, 260 km beyond Tim Missaou. This dusty village has little to offer the traveller, with the exception of a customs office and police station. The people are friendly here, however, and water is easily available. There is a petrol station, but getting fuel is like drawing blood from a stone, even if they have supplies. The track to the south-west of the village is signposted to Mali. Heading north-westwards, you join a 150 km sandy trail which takes you past the Kreb Bekateil Escarpment (marking the Mali/Algeria border) to Bordj Moktar. This is the best route if you are travelling back up to Reggane.

The journey north to Reggane leads through one of the most hazardous regions of the Sahara. Its danger lies in its size, and the occasional patches of very soft sand. The settlements in this huge expanse of flat gravel plain are about 900 km apart. There is one water reservoir in the middle, just north of the Tropic of Cancer. Consequently, this journey requires very careful preparation. A breakdown here could be disastrous. In summer the heat is intense and stifling, with temperatures in excess of 45° C (113° F). Despite the complete emptiness and isolation of the desert, this area is incredibly tranquil and beautiful, particularly at dawn and sunset. Walking a short distance from your vehicle, there will be nothing to see and nothing to hear.

Mali

If you intend to continue to Gao, be prepared for long periods of driving in soft sand. Tessalit is the first Malian town you reach –

A sand storm near the Malian border

150 km from Timeiaouine. On arrival, make sure that your papers are in order (visas, carnets, etc.). There is very little of interest here. Water is available, and fuel might be.

The piste to Gao is very sandy, so low-range gears are *de rigeur*. You will be lucky to see more than two other vehicles a day. Sand storms are a distinct possibility. They have a tendency to arise late in the day. A bulging wall of sand and dust – hundreds of metres high – turns the sky orange. Within seconds, you and your vehicle are engulfed. All you can do is stop and shut everything. The buffeting of the vehicle may go on for several hours. Rain then follows immediately after the dust storm.

Allow three days to make this journey. During this time, changes in vegetation will be apparent. The differences are linked to the gradual changes in weather patterns, as rain becomes more likely. Towards Gao, the amount of grassland increases, and the dry river valleys (*oueds*) may be luxuriantly vegetated in mid summer. These areas are grazed by camels and the ubiquitous goats. It is also one of the first areas since the northern oases in which there are obvious signs of wildlife.

Arriving in Gao, you will be greeted by a horde of laughing and shouting children who follow you into the centre. The town is composed of mud-brick buildings and nomads' tents. These are linked by streets often covered with thick, green sewage. The best base from which to explore Gao is the campsite that adjoins the town's only hotel, L'Atlantide. The camp is a meeting spot for travellers and European aid workers. It is the best place to learn of tried-and-tested routes through the desert, and to find out what is really happening in the western Sahara. When you get to Gao, check in with the police and customs. You may need special documentation if you intend to remain in Mali for several weeks. Check this beforehand if possible. Remember that you will have to make the 1,000 km journey to the capital, Bamako, if this is the case.

The people of Gao are delightful. The women wear very bright and colourful robes. There are few signs of poverty, and the shops are well stocked with food – from hot chocolate to tinned tomatoes. Gao's market is a riot of colour, from the people's clothing to the wide variety of exotic fruits and vegetables for sale. There are mangoes, melons, limes, oranges and spices galore. Meat is available in abundance, as are fresh and dried fish from the local river Niger. The only unappetising sight is the flies jostling for position on the meat!

As you move to the villages outside Gao, the poverty becomes more obvious. The Tamachek nomads live very simply, in circular mat tents. Their children come to Gao to beg for money and food, gently tugging at visitors' sleeves. Fourteen years ago, drought forced these nomads to live around Gao, so that they could earn enough money to buy cattle and return to their former way of life. Donations of grain from the West are of little use, when it is animals that they need.

Four hundred years ago, Gao was the centre of the huge Songhai empire. One of its emperors, Askia Mohammed Ture, lies in a large tomb in the north of the town.

The return journey from Gao can prove difficult if it is attempted early in the rainy season of late summer. North of Gao, the terrain becomes a quagmire. On the Michelin 153 map the road is described as impassable during the rainy season, so you would be well advised not to commence the northward journey too late. Heavily laden vehicles soon become bogged down. Searching for usable routes can become tiresome and very time-consuming. The oueds, which presented no problems a month earlier, can now be flowing with water.

From Tessalit, you continue to Bordj Moktar – once more in Algeria.

Reggane to Bechar

After crossing the Tanezrouft from Mali, or the desert from Ain Salah, the mud dwellings of Reggane are a welcome sight. Travel to the west is blocked by the largest dune system in the Sahara – the Erg Chech. The road north to Bechar passes through the area at which the Erg Chech and the Grand Erg Occidental meet. Consequently, this is the ideal route for those who want to see the classic, romantic Sahara. This endless sea of sand has waves hundreds of metres in height.

Reggane was once a large military outpost. It was developed by the French to serve as a nuclear testing site in the nearby desert. Algeria's independence brought the dismantling of the site. As a result, Reggane has an atmosphere of decay and gives the impression that it possesses more buildings than it needs.

A tarmac road leads north to Adrar, passing numerous *fogarra* irrigation systems. The local people face a never-ending task of fighting the encroaching mobile dunes. Adrar is a large administrative centre. Like Reggane, its characteristic red-mud buildings are Sudanese in style. Grand arches mark the gateway into the central square. It has most of the facilities you would expect of a large oasis town.

The tarmac road continues right through to Bechar. Happily, this means that less time need be spent worrying about the driving conditions. As a result, you can concentrate on enjoying this oasis-hopping journey. Beyond the Timimoun turning, the road is framed by erg on both sides. It follows a gravel valley which has been a route for nomads and camel caravans for centuries. Marked by stone pillars and buckets, wells are a common sight. (Water lies just below the surface.) Sandstorms are rarely a problem here. During early spring and late summer, however, the strong afternoon winds can be rather irritating.

The attractive northward journey will take you past a series of oases, scattered with dunes and date palms. You may care to make a detour to Timimoun, from the junction north of Adrar. The scenery is quite superb. Majestic ancient forts contrast with lush gardens – intricately irrigated to provide a wide range of fruit and vegetables.

Less than 30 km past the turning to Beni-Abbes, the road forks. The road to the west joins the Hammada du Draa route. This is under military control and is impassable. During earlier conflicts with Morocco, the border was littered with mines and traps. As a result, you must turn right to reach Bechar. This journey passes through the idyllic oasis of Taghit.

Taghit is set against a spectacular backdrop of sand dunes, that rise high above the village. The road deteriorates in places, and there is a steady increase in the amount of esparto grass and thorn bushes. Taghit is a classic *Beau Geste* village, with its fort and sand dunes. The clear water of the beautiful, palm-lined river supports an abundant oasis life. The huge Mauritanian toad is fairly common here, together with the usual entourage of croaking frogs.

The town of Bechar is relatively disappointing. So if you intend to stop in the Saoura region, Taghit is the best place in which to do so. With its concrete blocks of flats, Bechar is the largest town since Gao or Tamanrasset. It lies at the intersection of the Draa valley and the Tafilalt area of Morocco. In fact, it is a very short distance from the Saoura region to Erfoud and Rissani, on the other side of Erg Chebbi (see the section on Morocco). Unfortunately, the border dispute with Morocco means that it is almost impossible to cross the frontier here. Just north of Bechar, there is a crossing at Figuig, although it is normally closed. Consequently, if you want to get into Morocco, you have to make an extensive detour, via Oujda in the north.

Taghit – true Beau Geste country, with fort, palms, and sand dunes

The North-West

From Bechar, our route crosses the Saharan Atlas, before dropping down to Ain Sefra, which is just off the main road. This stretch of the journey is marked by numerous relics of the guerrilla warfare of thirty years ago. Kilometres of barbed wire and French-built concrete forts line the road. You are advised to keep well clear of the broken bottles that were laid under the sand to deter guerrilla crossings from Morocco.

The mountains here – Les Monts des Ksour – are some of the more interesting in the range. At an altitude of about 1,000 m , we are back to the cypress and poplar forests of the Atlas. There are a large number of rock paintings in the area – most off the road to El Bayadh. It is worth making enquiries about them in Ain Sefrah. Tiout lies on the N47, just outside Ain Sefrah. On a cliff-face here, there are paintings that depict the hunting of elephants, ostriches and buffaloes. Most of this work is believed to be more than 5,000 years old.

The scorpion, *Androctonus australis*, is said to be found along this stretch of mountains – as far as Ouargla. It is one of the most deadly species in the world.

Travel is comparatively easy in this area. There is a rail link with Oran, and all the roads are very good.

Driving north of Ain Sefrah, you return to a plateau of chotts. The main road to Oran passes through the desolate Chott Ech Chergui – a huge salt lake. This is usually dry, especially since the damming that has diverted much of the water that used to be found in this region.

Tlemcen and Oran

The minor road that leads through Tlemcen, to Oran, traverses a rich agricultural landscape of vineyards and olive groves. These are the wheatfields of Algeria.

Tlemcen is the fifth of the Maghreb's imperial cities. It is a beautiful town of mosques and minarets. Olives and pines intersperse the buildings, while vines grow over Islamic arches. The vines were originally grown so that the grapes could be eaten. The arrival of the French saw them diverted to wine-making. Tlemcen has dozens of historical monuments. The architecture of the mosques is particularly interesting. It derives from Islamic influences in Spain. Similar examples can be seen at Cordoba and Granada. The Great Mosque was built at the same time as its equivalent in Fes. The design of arcades and arches is common to both. If you want a good overall view of this beautiful countryside, then the best vantage point is the hill of Kalaa, which overlooks the city.

From Tlemcen, it is a short distance to the Moroccan border town of Oujda. This is the only point at which border crossing can be guaranteed. A road follows the border down to the coast at Marsa Ben-Mehidi. The small sandy bays and rocky cliffs make pleasant stops.

Oran is the second largest city in Algeria. With its international airport and industrial complexes, it is not as attractive as Algiers. After clearing Mostaganem, the coast road to Algiers offers some breathtaking views. To the south-east of Oran lies Mascara – set near wooded hills of oak, cypress and olive groves. The region is scattered with attractive gorges and remote valleys.

TUNISIA

The hard-capped mountains between Gabes and Kebili

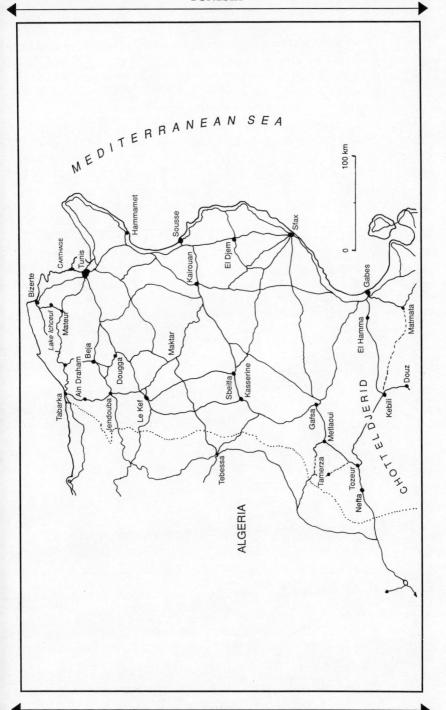

Introduction

Tunisia is the most accessible of the three countries which we describe in this book. It has an area of 165,000 sq. km and a population of around six million. The country is positioned as a wedge between Algeria and Libya, at the eastern limit of the Atlas mountains.

Tunisia offers a number of habitats for the naturalist to explore. These range from fertile hill country, through vast, intensively cultivated palmeries, to the astonishingly bleak, flat landscapes of the chotts.

Although relatively westernised, the cities of Tunisia contain much that is of interest. The monuments of Sousse and Kairouan are particularly impressive. Tunis itself is one of the most pleasant capital cities that one could wish to visit. Its humid summer climate is the only real drawback.

With its well-developed tourist infrastructure, Tunisia is an ideal introduction to north Africa. It will not, though, disappoint the traveller who is looking for something a little different.

Geography

Heading inland from Tunisia's north coast, the land swiftly climbs as you approach the Tell Atlas. Formed from clay, limestone and sandstone, these hills reach less than 1,000 m in height. To the east, along the Mediterranean coast, there is a fertile agricultural plateau. This also encompasses the main population centres and tourist resorts.

To the south of the country, you come across the chotts, a remarkable feature of Tunisia's geography. A chott is an inland salt flat. The largest of these is the Chott el Djerid.

Flora and Fauna

Tunisia's small size means that the wildlife is essentially Mediterranean in origin. Only as you reach the Chott el Djerid does the Saharan influence begin to dominate. The cork oak forests around Ain Draham, and the bird-rich Lake Ichceul are both important areas for the naturalist. Tunisia, with its large number of oases and central geographical position in north Africa, is an important migratory route for birds.

Climate

Spring is undoubtedly the best time at which to visit Tunisia. Not only is the botany at its most impressive, but the south of the country is not unpleasantly hot. In summer, you will find siestas especially attractive in places like Douz and Nefta. In July, the average temperature in Nefta is 32° C (89.6° F). Tunis can be unpleasantly hot and humid in the summer. In most other coastal settlements, the sea breeze takes the edge off the temperature. Note that 'seasonal' factors mean that hotels tend to be cheapest during the early and late parts of the year.

Driving in Tunisia

Tunisia has the best road network in north Africa. The high-quality, metalled routes reach most places that you will want to visit. They are rarely congested in rural areas. Petrol stations are fairly frequent. Minor roads tend to be little more than rocky tracks or marks across a sandy surface. Road conditions deteriorate significantly to the south of Matmata.

Maps

The Hildebrand Travel Map (1:900,000) is excellent. It also contains city plans and tourist information.

Currency

The Tunisian dinar is divided into 1,000 millèmes. Dinars can only be bought and sold inside Tunisia. There is also a restriction that you cannot convert back into sterling (or any other non-Tunisian currency) more than 30 per cent of the amount that you originally exchanged. You must therefore retain all your exchange receipts until you leave the country. Be careful not to exchange too much money.

Even in Tunis, it can be difficult to find a bank that has stocks of sterling. You may have to accept French francs, and then convert them again in the UK.

Credit cards are widely accepted in larger towns, but you may have problems with Eurocheques.

Language

Arabic is the official language, although French is very widely spoken. A growing number of people, especially in tourist areas, speak English. You may find students of the language asking you to talk to them in order that they can practise conversation.

The Sahel Coast

Kairouan

Getting there

If you want to take a louage from Tunis to Kairouan, you will have to make your way to the end of the Avenue de la Gare, furthest away from the Place Barcelone. The vehicles muster in a dusty carpark down to the left. The two-hour journey will set you back 5 dinars per person. Buses leave from a station south of the medina. Follow the Rue Jazira down from the Place de la Victoire, to the

The *Thymelaea* flower

Bab Jazira. From there, continue south to the end of the Rue Sidi el Bechir. (The terminus used for any given route has a tendency to change, so check when you get there. If you have gone to the wrong place then hop on to one of the urban buses which frequently run between the main termini.)

Once out of the capital, you join a motorway which leads 62 km south-west to a junction with the coast road, near the holiday resort of Hammamet. The journey begins by passing through a relatively verdant countryside of scrub-covered hills. After 30 km, the road passes the Djebel Ressas, to the right. This massive block of hard rock, sheer-sided and fringed by shallower slopes of scree debris, rises from the surrounding plain. Joining Route 1, the following 36 km afford glimpses of the sea to the left, while hills rise to the right.

Just north of Enfidaville, a junction offers the choice of staying close to the coast and making your way straight to the port/resort of Sousse, or heading inland to Kairouan. If time allows, it is well worth doing the latter. Leaving the coast, Route 2 passes through ordered plantations of olive trees. For much of the way, the road is fringed by tatty prickly pear bushes. As you pass the large lake, Sebkha Kelbia, and approach Kairouan itself, the trees give way to a featureless plain, largely devoid of vegetation.

As an alternative to the motorway and the coast road, you could head 78 km south of Tunis on Route 3. This brings you to the town of Fahs, where there is a Saturday market (convenient if you take the regular Friday flight from London to Tunis, by Tunis Air). Thuburbo Majus, an area of Roman ruins, lies 3 km to the north. While interesting, it certainly does not merit a special trip if you are planning to visit Dougga, Tunisia's main Roman site, anyway.

From Fahs, Route 3 continues for another 90 km, until it reaches Kairouan.

The Holy City of Kairouan

After Mecca, Medina and Jerusalem, Kairouan is the fourth holiest city for the adherents of Islamic religion. Some Moslems once believed that seven visits to the city would confer the same spiritual favour as the classic pilgrimage to Mecca. Although one might not think so, given the Kairouan's roasting summer climate, the location of this settlement was determined by divine intervention. Oqba Ibn Nafaa, a follower of the Prophet Mohammed, was leading his soldiers into conflict with the Berbers and the Byzantines, in the early 670s. Their spirits were raised by the discovery of a golden drinking vessel that had been lost in Mecca, and also by the sudden appearance of a holy spring at a point where Oqba's horse lost its footing. Cheered by these omens, Oqba founded his capital here.

The years of the Aghlabite Dynasty saw Kairouan develop into a city of great learning and monumental splendour. It was a focus of resistance to Bourguiba's attempts at secularisation, and even now remains an important religious centre. Now the fifth largest town in the country, Kairouan is a centre for the manufacture of cigarettes and carpets, as well as being a market for local agricultural produce.

Whether you arrive by louage or bus, you will be dropped off in the French New Town. There are plenty of rough-looking rotisseries at which to eat in this area. The food is quite acceptable, as long as you don't look too closely, and are relatively tolerant of chives! If you view discretion as the better part of valour, the New Town includes a couple of smart supermarkets at which you can stock up with provisions. Make your way north to the medina and find the large open space that stands by the Bab Ech Chouhada, at the meeting point of the Avenues Ali Belhouane and de Kortoba. The Bab consists of a pair of large archways in the well-restored city walls. With the tourist Office standing opposite the gates, this is an ideal centre from where to take your bearings. The Tourist Office, with its attractive collonaded pool, is a cool refuge in which to pick up information about Kairouan and to buy your ticket to the town's monuments (600 millèmes). It is open from 7.30 to 1.30 and 3.00 to 5.30. You can ring the Tourist Office on (07) 21797.

The cheapest hotels are to be found in the medina. Walk through the Bab Ech Chouhada, and along the Avenue Bourguiba – the main artery through the Old City. Within a couple of hundred metres you reach a raised, triangular café terrace. The road forks to each side. Taking either route and then, in a few metres, cutting back along the third side of the triangle of buildings, you will arrive at the Café Barouta. To its right, a doorway gives straight on to a staircase that leads up to the Hotel Barouta. Pleasant twin-bedded rooms look out over the Avenue Bourguiba, and over the rooftops of the medina. (In common with most Tunisian hotels, your bed will have a folded sheet lying at its foot, and a pillow with the soft, yielding feel of Cornish granite.) Strewn with rubbish and old food, the flat roofs are home to tens of mangy stray cats. You will pay about 2.5 dinars per person per night – very reasonable if you are not overly concerned by the state of the toilets. The hotel is ideally situated in the centre of the medina's bustle. As well as the sounds of people going about their daily business, the air is full of the squeaking strains of traditional Tunisian music. This provides a strange blend with the occasional tape of slightly dated Western music, the angry buzz of a moped or the eerie wailing of the muezzin. There is no more relaxing way to spend an evening than to sit on your window ledge, leisurely dismembering a water melon, while the scurrying activity of the day draws to a close beneath you.

Kairouan is an attractive, friendly and unforbidding place. The medina is small enough to explore without fear of getting lost. Rough, dusty and potholed roads contrast with housefronts that are often intricately decorated with latticework designs. The town's narrow streets support barbers, bakeries, rotisseries, sweetmeat stalls and shops selling carpets, clothing and leathergoods. Fabric shops are easy to locate, with their large bundles of brightly dyed woollen thread hanging outside. (Look out for a particularly good general store a few metres in through the Bab Ech Chouhada, on the left). The buildings, complete with peeling plaster, tatty awnings, corrugated iron and scaffolding, project a shabby yet welcoming air. Above street level, the whitewashed walls glare in the sunlight.

As you tour the monuments of Kairouan, you will have to tear off a marked section of your ticket at each one, and give it to the 'guardian' on duty. Generally, you will not find the sites too crowded, although you would be well advised to make an early start in order to avoid the coach tours which bus holidaymakers in from the coastal resorts.

Head over the square from the Tourist Office and through the Bab. Then follow the first alleyway to the right. In a few metres you will come upon a man sitting on a chair by a doorway. He will take a part of your ticket and usher you into the Zaouia Sidi Abd El Ghariani. You find yourself in a square atrium surrounded by a colonnade, with smaller, cool chambers leading off to the side. The floor is decorated in a starred pattern of black and white marble. The lower parts of the walls are covered with delicately and complexly painted tiles. The classic horseshoe shape figures prominently, most noticeably above the mihrab, where the curve of alternately black and white marble blocks is filled by stuccowork in the shape of a peacock's fan. The second floor of the atrium is largely wooden.

Leaving the zaouia, turn right and then take the first lane to the right. This brings you back to the southern wall of the medina.

Turn left and follow the wall as far as the Bab El Khoukha. From here, the Rue Ibrahim Ibn Aghlab leads straight to the Grand Mosque.

One tends to arrive at the Grand Mosque in the expectation of finding a riot of colour and involved decoration. Instead, much as when you enter the Duomo in Florence, you are faced by an impressive, yet surprisingly austere building. It seems more like a military stronghold than a place of worship. The courtyard is vast. In the middle, there are hollowed-out column bases which provide access to underground wells. Grooves are scored in their edges by the ropes used to haul water up to the surface. Tall buttressed walls run down either side of the courtyard. At one end there is a colonnade from which the minaret rises. It is a broad sturdy tower with three windows, topped with battlements and two narrower, carved levels. At the opposite end of the great open space is another colonnade, beneath which there are several doors into the main prayer hall. In the centre of the colonnade is one arch larger than the others, on top of which stands an octagonal storey, itself surmounted by a grooved, brick cupola. The windows beneath the dome are shaded by carved cedarwood shutters. Inside the prayer hall, rafia matting covers the floors and the lower parts of the columns. Huge, multi-layered chandeliers hang from the high ceiling, illuminating the ornate mihrab at the far end of the room.

After the Grand Mosque, the next monuments to which your ticket provides access are the ninth-century Aglhabid Pools. They are unique among the sights of Kairouan in that they are utterly missable. Buttresses extend into the green water that fills two circular reservoirs to the north of the town.

From the Grand Mosque walk along the northern section of the medina walls. The road leading to the kasbah is unremarkable, except for the number of persistent guides who run up to offer you their services. Beyond the kasbah, you find yourself in the Place de Tunis. This stands on the outer side of the Bab Tunis – the other end of the Avenue Bourguiba from the Bab Ech Chouhada. Assuming that you decide to forgo the delights of the Aghlabid Pools, you should carry on beyond the end of the medina wall, until you reach a T-junction with the Avenue Zama El Balaoui. Turning right you will soon come upon the Mosque of the Barber, at the point where the road bears sharp right.

The mosque gained its name from Abu Zama Balaoui, who is buried here. He became known as 'the Barber' because he used to carry three hairs from the Prophet's beard with him, wherever he went. It is perhaps the most beautiful of Kairouan's religious buildings. Outside the main gate of the mosque there is a crowd of souvenir sellers, preying on the occupants of the coaches that frequently stop here.

Crossing the main courtyard (where you will be supplied with a djellabah, if you happen to be showing too much leg) you pass through a small chamber, into a thin rectangular atrium. The green benches beneath the colonnade provide a cool vantage point from which to admire the plasterwork, dominated by an eight-pointed star pattern. Again we find the familiar combination of complicated, colourful mosaics and tiles, topped by white stuccowork. At the end of this passageway, you come into a small antechamber. The floor is a marble tessellation of hexagons and triangles. Directly overhead is the cupola. This is filled with ornate stuccoed plaster, unfortunately backlit by gaudy coloured lights. Beyond this room lies another courtyard, and the prayer hall. The mosaics around the courtyard are a dazzling frenzy of blues, greens and yellows. Marble columns support carved, pale-beige arches. Several women and children sit on the matting outside the hall. A contemplative, coughing guardian sits with them. Small birds perch on the green and white lamps that hang from the cedarwood roof of the colonnade. They are unworried by the noise of the women's sandals, clattering and sliding across the cool, hard paving stones. The shaded perimeter of the courtyard is the perfect location in which to spend an hour or so, meditating on the meaning of life!

Sousse

If you are travelling from Kairouan to Sousse without your own vehicle, then your best bet is make your way to the louage station opposite the PTT (post office). As with many towns in Tunisia, the pick-up point is a concealed yard – just ask when you get near. There is often a real crush for the cars to Sousse, but fortunately the bus service stops just a few metres along the road, so you should not have too long to wait for one or other.

The bus journey of 60 km costs a little over 1.5 dinars per person, and takes about 1¾ hours. Much of the route crosses a flat plain. This is largely barren, with a few fields delineated by prickly pear hedgerows. The monotony is broken by the occasional flock of sheep or plantation of olive trees.

Sousse is a delightfully attractive place in which to spend a couple of days. Although resort tourism is obviously a strong influence, the town is not unpleasantly crowded, especially if you manage to avoid coming at the end of July and beginning of August. The coastal location also takes the edge off the temperature.

This site has been regarded as important by all the various civilisations that have occupied northern Africa over the past three millennia. Believed to predate Carthage, the town was certainly flourishing by 800 BC. After the Carthaginian era, the Romans, Vandals and Byzantines all occupied Sousse. The Aghlabites used the port to serve Kairouan, and this brought prosperity to the town. During the ninth century, they built the monuments that are now the main features of the medina. In recent years, the combination of industry and a growing tourist trade have ensured Sousse's place as Tunisia's third city.

The buses stop beneath the vast walls of the medina. Make your way down the hill, past the colourful display of red, orange and mauve bushes, and into the Place Farhat Hached, which is essentially the centre of the town. Walk into the medina, and make your way around the left side of the Grand Mosque. The trinket-strewn Rue de Paris leads away into the centre of the old city. On the first two or three occasions that you make your way along this street you will be constantly assailed by shopkeepers offering their trendy leatherware, T-shirts, furry nylon camels and the like. You could do much worse than stay at the Hotel des Perles (number 71). Only the doorway is visible from the outside. This leads along a corridor to a television room and an intermittently operating shower (250 millèmes per go.) The bedrooms are upstairs. They are clean, which again cannot be said for the toilets. At 2.5 dinars per person, however, you are not going to find anywhere with an avocado-green bathroom suite and freshly unwrapped bar of Camay!

To visit the Grand Mosque, you will have to buy a 900 millème ticket from the guardian, who sits in the shade 50m away from the main gate. (The mosque is open every morning, except Fridays.) Entering through a gate beneath the battlements, you find yourself in an attractive, colonnaded courtyard. A single line of Koranic inscription runs above the arches. The floor of the yard is a pattern of concentric rectangles – alternately standard slabs and crazy paving with purple mortar. In one corner, a broad staircase leads up to the battlements, near the squat, round, eleventh-century minaret. Large, polished, wooden doors lead into the prayer hall, the entrances to which are roped off. Glimpses of the interior reveal little ornamentation. Matting covers the floors, while small jugs stand by each of the columns.

The Ribat is only a few metres away from the mosque. The building functioned as a cross between a monastery and a fort – housing religiously motivated warriors. Admission (all day, every day except Mondays) costs 800 millèmes. If you want to take photographs, this costs an extra 2 dinars, which is certainly worth it. Cells lead off from the 'cloister' that surrounds the main courtyard. Nosing around the cells, you will find that they have been used to store some of the carved stonework that once adorned the ribat. Steps lead up to the second level. Again a series of cells lead off from the walkway, each with a small niche or alcove in one wall. Directly over the entrance, on this second level, stands the prayer hall. In contrast with the mosques, the hall is open to visitors. The room is almost crypt-like. Its narrow, slit windows show that the exterior walls are nearly two metres thick at this point. The window apertures are wider on the inside of the wall than on the outside. Consequently, they admit a surprising amount of light.

Climbing up to the level of the battlements, the wide walkway gives good views over the town. A chamber over the main gate has large holes in the floor from where things could be dropped on attackers. (Be careful not to let children wander in here unattended.) Finally, make your way up the dark, claustrophobic, spiral staircase that leads up through the minaret. The top affords superb photo-opportunities over the Grand Mosque, the old city, the port and the new hotels.

The streets of the medina, near the Ribat and the Grand Mosque, are confusing, yet unintimidating. Wandering through them, you never know what waits around the next corner. Small shops sell ironwork, brassware, carpets, leather, bright clothing and numerous wooden items. The air is thick with the sickly smell of olives and spices. Amused boys gaze at vast barrowloads of snails, as one or two occupants make a ridiculously slow attempt to escape. Malodorous cows' heads hang from hooks – their eyes shut and their mouths stuffed with an artistically arranged handful of herbs.

Other than the sight of the container ships illuminated in the night, the port area contains little of interest. There are, though, some good restaurants nearby, several of which naturally specialise in seafood. On your way to eat in the evening, look out for the thousands of swallows that swoop around the city walls in the fading light.

The Avenue Habib Bourguiba leads from the Place Farhat Hached to the main beach. This is the most touristy stretch in the town. Amidst the cafés, nightclubs and hotels, the ghastly cuddly camels are much in evidence alongside postcards and badly screen-printed T-shirts. During the evening you can sip your outrageously overpriced Coca-Cola at a roadside table. Off-season this can verge on the pleasant, but it is highly avoidable in August. The same can be said for the vast swathe of sand that stretches northwards along the coast. The water here is warm, but reputedly polluted.

Sfax

Getting there

The buses south to Sfax leave from the station near the Bab Djerid gate. The journey costs 3.2 dinars per person, and lasts some 2½ hours. There is also a train service which runs six times a day.

The well-preserved amphitheatre at El Djem

Route 1 heads directly south from Sousse, through a well-cultivated landscape of olive trees. As the road continues, look out for the mini-gorges that have been eroded by the oueds. Just over 60 km from Sousse you will see the town of El Djem, dominated by its remarkable third-century amphitheatre, rising from an otherwise featureless plain. This is the sixth largest such arena in the world, and it is one of the best preserved. The damage that has been sustained could even be regarded as an improvement, as it provides a cross-section of the building's design. Animals, in plentiful supply in Africa, played an important part in entertaining the 30,000 people who could be accommodated by the amphitheatre. In the years since the Romans left, the arena has frequently found itself used as a stronghold for assorted rebellious groups.

'The most beautiful city in the world'

When the author Ronald Firbank described Sfax in these glowing terms, he must surely have been suffering from temporary delirium. This is one of the most missable settlements in Tunisia. We describe the town because many people will choose to break their journey from Sousse to the deep south here, not because it has much to recommend it as a destination in its own right.

Having struggled their way through miles of sprawling, and often wealthy, suburbs, the buses from Sousse drop you outside the railway station, at the far end of the Avenue Habib Bourguiba. Walking along the avenue, you will find yourself in a pleasant, yet uninspiring French new town. The most attractive feature, perhaps, is the range of alarmingly tempting patisseries which lurk around every corner. When you reach the impressive clock tower, that stands above the town's Archaeological Museum, turn right and make your way along the Boulevard de la Republique. The boulevard leads to the Bab Diwan – the main gateway into the medina.

The Bab consists of two large arches in the high, crenellated and heavily restored city walls. A bustle of people and vehicles flow through them from dawn to dusk. Just inside, there is a cluster of food stalls and shops. Bread and fruit dominate. Turning sharp right and then quickly left, you find yourself climbing up the Rue Mongi Slim, the main route through the medina. The narrow street is lined with shops, rotisseries and hotels, but it fortunately lacks the persistent hawkers of Sousse. Rue Mongi Slim is your best bet to find somewhere cheap in which to stay. Try the Hotel El Jemiaa (number 37). Only the doorway is visible from the road. It leads straight to a stairway that takes you up to the reception area/TV room. The proprietor, Mohsen Ben Tahar Mesfar, is a friendly chap, who charges about 2 dinars per person per night.

Numerous side-streets and covered souks lead away from the Rue Mongi Slim. Fabric shops and tailors are especially common, while some of the souks are overflowing with rug and carpet sellers. The Grand Mosque, in the midst of the alleys of the medina, is not easy to locate. The huddle of the surrounding buildings makes it almost impossible to get a good view of the whole mosque. Even so, by walking around the perimeter, you should be able to catch several interesting glimpses of the interior.

At the far end of the Rue Mongi Slim, another Bab leads out on to a large market complex – an attractive example of modern brick and stone vaulting. This is a fascinating area to wander around. Make your way past the sacks of beans, pulses and spices, and the plastic crates of fruit and vegetables, to the small fish market at the far side. Beware, though, of small children who have a disconcerting tendency to rush up and thrust some repulsively malodorous dead sea creature in your face, in a bid to sell it before the corpse degenerates into a condition in which it attempts a getaway of its own accord.

The Saharan Fringe

The East

Gabes

The bus from Sfax to Gabes leaves from outside the railway station. Rather than paying on the bus, you have to buy your ticket from a small office on the other side of the road. While you wait to depart (the main morning service leaves at 11), you can sit on the pavement and enjoy a cassecroute from the jovial stallholder. Once the bus arrives, you will find departure delayed for as long as it takes his son to deliver food orders to any hungry travellers on board. If you want something to eat that is less of an intestinal gamble, there is a small shop on the left-hand side of the Gare de Sfax which sells biscuits (as well as newspapers and postcards).

The bus journey to Gabes reputedly takes two hours, although we have never managed it in under three. There is little to be said about the 140 km stretch of Route 1, as it hugs the coast of the Gulf of Gabes – olive plantations tend to lose their novelty value after a while!

A vast palmery is the first thing you see of Gabes. There are over a quarter of a million trees in the few square kilometres to the north of the town. Their quality, though, is affected by the moist, salty atmosphere of the coastal strip.

The bus station stands in the western corner of the town. To find a hotel, you will have to follow the Avenue Farhat Hached for some distance, and then cut across to the Avenue Habib Bourguiba. We found Gabes the most difficult town in Tunisia in which to find a room during early summer. You will have to be prepared to make several attempts, and to pay quite a high price. Try the Hotel de la Poste. Its entrance is down a side-road, next to the Café de la Poste, on the Avenue Habib Bourguiba. Some persistence, and the adoption of an expression of resigned misery, may be required before a room is forthcoming. If successful, however, you will have a large room, with a single and a double bed, for 6 dinars. There are showers which work intermittently, and the toilets even flush! The principal drawback to this hotel is its proximity to a nearby mosque. Sleep is impossible before 11 at night, by which time the tape of the muezzin's evening call to prayer will have run its screeching course. There are food shops and a patisserie all within 100 m or so of the hotel.

The square in the centre of Gabes, opposite the Hotel Regina on the Avenue Habib Bourguiba

The Tourist Office stands at the western end of the Avenue Habib Bourguiba. At this point, the Avenue converges with the Boulevard Mohammed Ali and the Avenue Farhat Hached, to form the Avenue Habib Thameur. It then leads straight past the two main 'resort' hotels of Gabes, to the Casino Gabes Hotel/ Restaurant. This is a cool, relatively inexpensive and tackily decorated spot in which to have a meal. The chicken and chips plus salad is as good as you will find anywhere, although the chef's enthusiasm for chillis and hot onions may not be to everyone's taste. The restaurant cat certainly has no complaints about the food, judging by the enthusiasm with which it attempts to extract tangible sympathy from soft-hearted diners.

The restaurant opens out on to the beach. To the left a breakwater of boulders forms one arm of the port. The port is largely used to serve a fishing fleet, but there are usually a few general cargo vessels berthed as well. To the right, a sandy beach stretches into the distance. The water and sand are both fairly dirty, while the tides often bring in cuttlefish and sponges, tangled up in vast quantities of seaweed. It is hard to believe that the tourists in the expensive hotels, Chems and Oasis, find that Gabes beach lives up to brochure-inspired expectations.

Heading to the end of the Avenue Habib Bourguiba furthest from the sea, you come upon the Grand Djara. This is a lively market area, open quite late into the evening. Further out is is a stagnant river that separates the town from the palmery.

Chenini

The village of Chenini lies a couple of kilometres to the west of Gabes. It is a favourite excursion for the tourist coaches. Nonetheless, this intriguing oasis habitat is undoubtedly worth a visit. There is plenty to explore by venturing just slightly off the beaten track. Getting to the village is easy. With your own vehicle it takes just a few minutes, while buses leave on the hour. The departure point is opposite the school on the Rue Jilani Labib. As you walk along the Avenue Farhat Hached, you can spot the road by looking out for a large sign for the Hotel Medina, on the left. It is just before the main bus station. The trip only takes 20 minutes and costs 170 millèmes.

The bus leaves you on a ridge overlooking a fertile scene below. A vast oasis area is sunk beneath the level of the surrounding, barren plain. Green palms and colourful bushes contrast with the dusty cliffs at the far side of the oasis, and the dull, brown flatlands beyond. The palm-filled gorge stretches around in an arc to the left. Scattered among the palms are the white-roofed chalets of the Club Chella. Despite the scruffy accommodation, the shaded open-air bar is an agreeable haunt at which to while away the hottest hours of the day, in the company of an overpriced beer. You may also be able to persuade the management to offer you use of the inviting swimming pool.

A road leads down from the ridge, with the Club to the left. Walking to the right, there is a path which leads out into the oasis. Large caves are hollowed out of the soft rock which rises up to the right of the path. After five minutes or so, the path starts to follow the course of a small stream. Small fish dart through the water, while pink flowers rise up on either side of the stream. Climbing up and away from the stream, you can appreciate the spectacular gorge scenery that has been eroded from the sandstone over the centuries. You will notice that the vegetation becomes sparse as soon as you move just a short distance away from the water. Animals, likewise, are few and far between. Sharp eyes may catch sight of a lizard flitting from rock to rock. If you do not see one running free, then rest assured that a small child will soon appear from nowhere and attempt to sell you one he caught earlier.

Matmata

Buses to Matmata leave from the main bus station at 7.00, 10.30, 12.00, 2.30 and 4.00. The journey takes a little over an hour, and costs 1 dinar. With your own vehicle, simply head south from Gabes on Route 107. Leaving the town behind, this route makes its way through an undulating, arid countryside. Mini-gorges, formed by the erosive power of small, seasonal streams can be seen time and time again. Occasionally a larger palmery or oasis will add a touch of welcome green to an otherwise brown semi-desert. Another familiar sight on this stretch of road is the marabout – a small, whitewashed, beehive-shaped tomb.

Thirty kilometres brings you to the dull village of New Matmata. From here onwards the landscape becomes much more hilly, as you make your way up into the Demer Mountains. With its large, scrub-scattered hummocks, this is a wonderfully impressive part of the country. One kilometre from Matmata itself, a ghastly hillside pastiche of the 'HOLLYWOOD' sign picks out the words 'WELCOME' and 'BIENVENUE' in white stone. This is an unfortunate indication of the degree to which the town has become subordinate to the demands of pasteurised tourism.

The region around Matmata, Tunisia's most famous troglodyte village

Matmata is Tunisia's most famous troglodyte village. The Berbers here live in dwellings dug from the sandstone. They originally came from the region of El Hamma, some 40 km to the northwest, before being forced south by Arab invaders in the tenth century. As you climb over a ridge and descend into the valley in which Matmata nestles, the view of the village is quite unique. The outlines of tens of large craters can be seen all around. Few buildings rise above ground level. Most of these are souvenir shops, serving the hordes disgorged from the vast air-conditioned coaches that frequently rumble their way in from the coast.

Despite the tourist development, Matmata is well worth the trip. Wandering through the valley, you will soon find a family that have opened their house up for visitors. (Expect to make a small donation of cigarettes.) Most of these subterranean dwellings are built on the same pattern. An entrance tunnel, in which animal fodder is stored, leads down to the main circular courtyard. Further small caves fan out from this central, open area. These small chambers are used as bedrooms, animal quarters etc. There will often be two storeys of these little caves.

In between the large craters formed by the central courtyards, the vegetation in Matmata is fairly sparse. It is limited to olive trees, fig trees, palms and the ubiquitous thorny scrub. With regard to the animal life, the most obvious inhabitants are the camels, of which a large number are used to transport the tourists around the village. Somewhat less photogenic, but interesting nonetheless, are the scorpions and the bats. Large ants are also common. Goats are not an unusual sight in the entrance passageways of Matmata's underground houses.

As you wander around this bizarre landscape, remember that not everyone here welcomes visitors with open arms. Several of the craters are surrounded with barbed wire. It is important to respect the privacy of those simply trying to carry on their daily lives without undue distraction.

Having spent some time exploring this parched location, you may well feel in need of refreshment. About 300 m along the road to Toujane, you come across the Hotel Marhala. (This is where the famous disco scene from *Star Wars* was filmed.) The hotel is built in the same fashion as the houses, with a network of courtyards spawning kitchens, bars and dining rooms in all directions. Concreted floors, electric power and whitewashed walls and ceilings are the only real concessions to outside civilisation. The bar is a splendidly cool resting place in which to recuperate from the blistering heat outside. Drinks aside, it is well worth visiting the Marhala, just to see the barman. *Fawlty Towers* may never seem unreal again!

Buses to Gabes depart from a dusty yard halfway up the main hill road out of town. They leave at 7.30, 9.00, 4.00 and 5.00.

If you have your own vehicle, then you would do well to cut short your visit to Matmata, and spend some time in Haddej. The village is signposted at a junction 4 km back along the Gabes road. Turning right at the junction will bring you, in 3 km or so, to this small settlement. Despite damage from flooding, Haddej gives a good indication of what life in Matmata was like before the arrival of the coaches and the film crews.

The Djerid

Douz and the Djebel Tebaga

Leaving the Mediterranean coast at Gabes, Route 16 cuts its way east, towards the Algerian border. The scenery, the settlements and the natural history of the interior are markedly different from the populous, prosperous coast.

Camels grazing on the plain between Gabes and Kebili

Buses run regularly from Gabes to Douz (although you may need to change at Kebili, about 1¾ hours into the journey). They leave the bus station on Avenue Farhat Hached at 8.30, 12.00 and 3.00. The fare to Douz is 3 dinars.

El Hamma lies 40 km west of Gabes. If you have time to stay here for longer than it takes to fill up with petrol, you could follow the example of the Romans and sample the thermal baths. They stand opposite the market square. For a small sum, you can relax on stone seats in a shallow pool of hot water. A high tolerance of sulphur, however, is a definite requirement!

El Hamma is the last settlement of any real size, until Kebili, 85 km to the west. This part of Route 16 is fast and largely devoid of traffic. It follows the course of a huge range of mountains – the Djebel Tebaga. The road runs parallel, and to the north, although there is a longer route of much lower quality that runs to the south. This should not be attempted without a four-wheel-drive vehicle. If you decide to try it, take a track leading off to the left, a couple of kilometres beyond El Hamma. You will finally emerge just south of Kebili, on the road to Douz.

The main road from El Hamma to Kebili runs along a flat pene-plain. The Djebel Tebaga rise dramatically to the left in a huge ridge. Several of the peaks are flat-topped blocks of rock that have proved more resistant to erosion than the surrounding areas. Other than the mountains, the landscape is largely semi-desert with some stabilising scrub and thorn bushes. Glasswort is fairly common at a number of places along the route. Ornithologists may spot an occasional lark or great grey shrike.

As the oasis of Kebili draws closer, from the angle at which the trees are bent over no doubt is left as to the direction of the prevailing wind. The countryside is often obscured by the loose sand whipped up in the frequent gusts. This soon generates an enveloping sandy haze that creates an eerie atmosphere with the curiously eroded sandstone.

The road to Douz passes straight through Kebili. There is no need to stop off here unless you have to, as this administrative centre contains little of interest. It is hard to imagine that this was a flourishing slave market a little over a hundred years ago.

On the other side of Kebili, the landscape is initially well-vegetated, with eucalyptus especially abundant. Together with the numerous palms, these thin out by the time you reach the small, picturesque village of Djemma, 16 km to the south. There are several distinct palmeries on route.

A view northwards across the sand dunes to the east of the Kebili to Douz

Near Douz, a wall of dead palm leaves is used to prevent too much sand drifting into the paths of vehicles. This forms a high dune to the east of the road. It is worth stopping and walking over to this ridge of sand. From the top, there is a good view over a lake in the clay, around which palms stand amidst the dunes. A brief examination of the sand will reveal the tracks of numerous animals, including beetles, jerboas and fennecs. Butterflies can often be seen, especially among the glassworts. Exposed chunks of desert rose are very common in the strip of wind-blown sand between the road and the ridge.

Douz stands just over 10 km south of Djemma. It instils an immediate impression of a settlement involved in a continuous and intractable battle with the Sahara. All the streets are simply sandy tracks, while the colour of most of the buildings does little to distinguish them from the dunes that surround the town. Douz is a friendly town that has grown quite noticeably in recent years. The former dearth of cheap accommodation is no longer such a problem. The Hotel Essaada is just 50 m away from the bus stop, and costs only 2 dinars a night. When you are shown your room, do not shake the bed-clothes, as the resulting cloud of sand may well suffocate its occupants. The hotel is fairly new. Indeed they may well have finished building the second floor by the time you get there!

A more expensive option is the Hotel Saharien, which will set you back 7.700 dinars for bed and breakfast, or 9.350 with an evening meal. Walk out along the road past the radio tower, and turn left after walking through the oasis for about a quarter of an hour. During the high season, the Saharien becomes almost unbearably touristy, but it is a pleasant stop if you come during the spring.

Douz (when not accompanied by a sandstorm) is an impressive and unique place to visit. Try to get here on a Thursday when the town square is thronged with people from nearby oases, trading food and clothing at the weekly market. The inhabitants are some of the friendliest you will meet in Tunisia. You can easily spend half an hour chatting over a glass of citronade in one of the town's cafés. For dinner, try the Restaurant 20 Mars, where the owner's two sons rustle up a tasty plate of brochettes, fried egg, salad and chips, with mint tea to follow.

The desert scenery that surrounds the town offers some attractive photo-opportunities, especially at dawn and dusk. A few words of caution, though. As in many places throughout the country, Western visitors will soon find themselves the object of the attention of local children. Their demands for presents can be firmly but politely refused, and this will usually be the end of the matter. If, however, a large group starts to gather, it is best to put away the camera and move off. Otherwise the common experience of having a small pebble shied in your direction, can develop into several people hurling sizeable stones. If you do come under attack in this fashion, make your way towards the nearest house or group of adults – somewhere that the youths will not risk throwing anything.

For dawn photographs, you will have to make your way along the road towards Ksar Ghilane. Past the newly built secondary school, the road disappears into a desert of low dunes with scrubby vegetation. Darkling beetles are a not-uncommon sight here, and their tracks even more so. Interestingly, if you pick one of these beetles and move it, they will always turn around and head off in the direction of the rising sun. Watch your step in this area, as there are several vehicle wrecks half-buried in the sand, together with the ghoulish spectacle of dried-out animal remains.

Along the southern margins of the oasis, sand grouse can be seen flying in from the desert to collect water for their young. A true desert species, it flies in small flocks to the oasis to soak its feathers with water. It can then carry the water back to the nest. The palms here are planted in rows and with enough spacing to

Date palms in the Douz oasis

allow additional crops to be grown below. Alfalfa is the most wide-spread crop and many birds come to feed on it. The resident desert sparrows nest in the tops of the palms and feed within the palmeries. During the spring and autumn these are joined by a host of migratory species: Chiffchaffs, bee-eaters, wagtails, flycatchers and warblers. The Moussier's redstart is a unique bird of northern Tunisia but does not move to these oases during the winter. Most of the palm trees have small wasp's nests attached several metres above the ground.

The Chott El Djerid

An 18-person minibus leaves Douz at 8.00 every morning, on a direct run to Tozeur, just over 120 km away to the north-west. Make sure that you reach the bus-stop in good time, as this is a particularly crowded service. Having retraced the track to Kebili, you rejoin Route 16. The bus makes several stops in the next 15 km, until crammed to capacity with passengers, it heads out over the chott.

The Chott El Djerid is the biggest of the salt lakes of the Sahara. It covers an area of over 5,000 sq. km. Crossing the chott used to be a hazardous endeavour (and impossible outside the summer months). If vehicles deviated from the recommended path there was a serious danger that they would break through the thin crust and sink into the mud below. Fortunately, the army have now built a metalled road across the chott, which means that it can be negotiated safely all year round.

Driving over this vast expanse is a strange experience. The roadway is raised a couple of feet above the chott. The flat surface of cracked mud glistens with the crystals of a thin salt crust. To the right of the road the salt and mud extend for several kilometres, until finally a spectacular mountain ridge rises up above the shimmering mirages. For much of the way, a 'stream' runs parallel to the road. The green-grey water is edged with glinting crystals of salt. In some places, the salt crystals have grown on each other to produce intricately patterned islands.

Understandably, there is little evidence of human activity on the chott. There are, though, a couple of cafés that seem to appear from nowhere. Small children play football on a shining pitch that stretches as far as the eye can see. The only vehicles to be seen off the road are water carriers, supported by vast balloon tyres.

Once over the salt flats, the road climbs up from sea-level and heads south-eastwards through a region thick with palms. After the hamlet of Kriz, the first settlement to appear is Degache. There is a campsite here, as well as a swimming pool. Tozeur, an erstwhile Roman frontier town, lies a further 10 km away.

Tozeur is the main administrative centre of this part of Tunisia. Historically, it owes much of its prosperity to the harvest from the date palms. The hillside town is quite picturesque, with decorative geometrical brickwork to be found on its main minarets and other buildings. The concern with decoration is obvious if you walk through the Ouled El Hadef, a part of the town dating from the fourteenth century. The massive oasis, with nearly a quarter of a million palms, is also worth a look, although less so if you are planning to head out to Nefta. There is a Tunis Air office in the town if you need to confirm your return flight. (The buses for Nefta leave from outside the station opposite the PTT.)

Nefta

Nefta stands 23 km to the west of Tozeur. The drive takes half an hour or so, past the airport and across a stretch of arid, barren desert. To the left, there is a good view down to the gleaming chott below. The entrance to the town is marked by an ornamental arch.

Nefta, once a Roman settlement, is now an important place of pilgrimage for the Sufi Moslems. Cheap accommodation is unfortunately not abundant. Try the Touring Club Hotel Marhala, overlooking the huge palmery from the Avenue Habib Bourguiba. It looks like a patterned, brick warehouse from the outside, but is attractive and comfortable on the inside. The rooms are spread around a central atrium, which is open to the sky. There is a prettily tiled pool in the middle, but this has always been empty when we have visited! A twin-bedded room will set you back 4.100 dinars per person, including breakfast (French-style coffee, with ageing bread and jam). The rooms have a shower and washbasin, and relatively comfortable beds (made from stone). The only drawback is the ventilation grille open to the air outside – when the wind gusts in the wrong direction it carries a cloud of sand in with it.

Down the hill from the hotel, a massive palmery extends over to the fringe of the Chott el Djerid. This swathe of green covers an area of over 1,000 hectares, encompassing nearly 400,000 trees. A number of tracks lead down from the road and make their way through the vast plantation, shaded by the fronds up above. A series of concrete channels carry water from a variety of natural springs and man-made wells, in order to irrigate the oasis. An alphanumeric coding system is painted on these channels, dividing the palmery into a series of individual *jardins*, each tended by a person or family. The palms are single sexed plants. Out of a group of 100 palms the owner will only keep one male tree. This will produce enough pollen for the 99 female trees. When the male flower ripens, the owner carefully picks it and pollinates the female flowers.

It is only by walking along one of the many tracks that you realise that there is more to the oasis than palms alone. In the most intensely cultivated areas, a system of 'six-tier farming' is adopted. The tall date palms provide shade for pomegranate trees, which in turn protect oranges. Closer to the ground, barley and broad beans provide shelter for onion plants. The palms, which are forty years old on average, have their dates harvested in October. On your way back up to the hotel, look out for the small marabout on the edge of the oasis.

The drainage and irrigation channels, which are constantly being diverted and rediverted, are home for crustaceans and snails as well as irritating insects. This forms the diet of a number of water birds, many of which are migratory. Egrets, storks, waders

The Nefta oasis with Chott el Djerid in the background stretching to the horizon

and the glossy ibis can be seen in the quieter parts of the oasis. Most of the oases are similar in their flora and fauna. See the Douz section, p.158 for further species.

The most photographed view of Nefta is that looking over the Corbeille. Leaving the Hotel Marhala, turn left along the Avenue Habib Bourguiba, and then take the first right. This dusty road curves around the edge of the town. When it reaches the carpark of the Mirage Hotel, go in and make your way over to the Café de la Corbeille. It affords a superb panorama over the Corbeille (or 'basket'). This is a huge, terraced basin filled with palms, fig and pomegranate trees and natural springs. (There is a hot spring directly below the café.) On the far side stands the old town, its skyline speckled with the whitewashed domes of mosques and marabouts. If possible, try and get here just as the sun is setting, when it imparts a golden glow to the town and the rocks alike. If you have your own vehicles, they can be left a short distance further along the road from the café, just before the road sweeps round to the left. Near here you will find plenty of drivers offering to take you for a tour in their horse and cart. Most will take you to an area of dunes, just to the north-west of the town, along the road to the Algerian border.

If you want to eat out in Nefta, make your own way east from the hotel, along the Avenue Habib Bourguiba. There a couple of restaurants on the hill beyond the Place de la Republique. We have heard good reports of the Restaurant Les Sources – it certainly cannot be worse than the Restaurant des Sportifs.

Returning along the main avenue, take a right hand turning at the Place de la République, and make your way into the old town. Up towards the Corbeille, columns of smoke rise from the brickery. Circular kilns are built into the ground. Palm fronds and trunks are pushed into a fire at the bottom of the kiln, from a pit. Recently fired bricks are stacked in piles nearby, ready for collection. The surrounding area is far from prosperous. Apparently ownerless chickens run loose, while green-tinged open sewers run down the dirt hills. The Place de l'Independence is the centre of this part of town, and best not visited alone and late at night.

The road from Nefta continues to the Algerian border. The desolation is almost tangible, as the road leaves the palmerie, overlooking the huge expanse of the chott.

Gafsa and the Mountain Oases

The bus from Nefta to Gafsa leaves from the front door of the Hotel Marhala. (It goes all the way to Tunis.) The fare to Gafsa is 2.900 dinars. If you take your own vehicle, drive back along Route 16, to Tozeur, and then head north on Route 3. The road passes through an avenue of eucalyptus, beyond which lies nothing but salt steppe. A short stop is worthwhile in order to appreciate the surprising variety of plant life. After a period of wet weather the region blooms with pink, blue and yellow flowers. The only permanent vegetation is a type of broom that can tolerate being buried by wind-blown sand. A series of small dunes have become built up around the forked broom plants. Jerboas and darkling beetles burrow in to these, while the broom supports the sand. There is also a population of chou-fleur here. This slow-growing plant has tightly packed leaves to reduce waterloss. Where they have been exposed to the wind, they stand like trees with miniature trunks.

Less than 10 km away, you reach the oasis town of El Hamma du Djerid. Like its namesake near Gabes, this settlement was well-known in Roman times for the therapeutic qualities of its hot springs. From here you can either continue along the main road to Metlaoui or divert to the mountain oases of Chebika and Tamerza.

Scrub desert of brooms and chou-fleur, between Tozeur and Metlaoui

The latter alternative is of very poor quality in places and may be better reached from Metlaoui.

Chebika and Tamerza

These two oases lie close to the Algerian border and are worth the detour from the main route. From El Hamma the road crosses the Chott Gharsa, climbing steadily through the barren, yellow hills to the gorge of Chebika. This has been carved out by the torrents of water that only rarely descend from the high mountains behind. The oasis is based around a freshwater stream that issues from a cascade near the old village (away from the new settlement). The palmerie lies within the picturesque gorge. A small dark snail is found in very dense numbers within the stream and this is food for the visiting waders. Tamerza is quite similar with a high waterfall, but it also has a hotel. Both of these areas remain unspoilt.

By day trumpeter finches with their peculiar whistle drink at the water's edge. They are very distinctive with their large red beaks, used for crushing dry seeds. Just outside the oases spurge plants are common with the attendant larvae of the Spurge hawkmoth. Marsh frogs croak throughout the night.

The conditions are very pleasant here in the mountains. The slightly less intense sun allows a longer flowering time. The thistle-heads are visited by a horde of pollinating insects including the large speckled cockchafer and a huge dark wasp with yellow spots on the abdomen. This latter species is common across the north African region and is semi-parasitic, laying its eggs on beetle larvae.

The road continues through the mountains to the mining town of Redeyef and Moulares, eventually descending to Metlaoui.

Metlaoui

Metlaoui lies 51 km away from Tozeur, across a steppe plain traversed by the El-Melah and Seldja rivers. These are rarely dry, so reeds and grasses thrive. Herons and buzzards can often be found feeding in the area. The crested lark is very common around the roadsides. Black wheatear can also be seen on posts or flying across the road. They are jet black, except for a white rump and tail.

The town of Metlaoui is dominated by the phosphate-mining industry. Consequently it only merits a petrol/soft drink stop. (There is also a Banque de Sud.) Metlaoui's situation, nestling at the foot of a mountain range, is nonetheless impressive. The Gafsa road runs parallel to this range, with a further set of pink phosphate hills to the south. Much of this area has been exhaustively mined, as the huge, dark spoil heaps indicate. The area does, however, have a certain fascination and a drive up into the mountains can be very rewarding. During the summer months there is a train which takes visitors up to the cooler region around Moulares and Redeyef. The road slowly winds up through hills of varying colour. Black kites and vultures soar in the sky, while the white-crowned black wheatear hunts on the ground. As you might guess, this species is similar to the black wheatear mentioned above, except that it has a white patch on its head. Vegetation is sparse here, boasting little more than tussocks of esparto grass and yellow-flowered cistus. The burrows of small mammals lead into what appears to be solid rock. The commonest species is the omnivorous spiny mouse. Be warned that ticks are very common here (mainly on the mouse!) and can easily be seen crawling over the rocks.

It is along this semi-desert region between Metlaoui and the mountain oases that you may come across the spiny-tailed lizard (*Uromastyx acanthinurus*). It can grow to over half a metre with a vicious-looking spiky tail. However, it is harmless and is considered lucky to see one. Local children regularly seem to keep them as

The road from Metlaoui to Moulares

pets. They normally spend the heat of the day in burrows, coming out early and late in the day. The fat tail stores food so that it can survive periods without eating.

Gafsa

Gafsa itself is a busy, frenetic town. It is the capital of south-western Tunisia and is an important centre for the phosphate industry. For somewhere to stay, try the Hotel Tunis, which is only a short walk from the bus station. You will pay 2.500 dinars per night for a basic room without a washbasin. The hotel is a favoured watering-hole for Tunisians who are studying English at night-school. Befriending tourists offer the opportunity of conversational practice.

A few metres from the hotel, the Restaurant du Carthage offers a reasonable mixed grill. Stalls out on the roadside sell a large range of fruit, vegetables and other food. Beware, though. Bottled mineral water is relatively scarce in the town.

The most popular tourist sights in Gafsa are the Piscines Romaines. These are two, rectangular Roman pools. The bottom of each pool is formed by natural rock, while the walls are built from large masonry blocks. In the smaller, a set of steps leads down to a platform, from where young show-offs leap into the water in an attempt to splash passers-by. A further set of steps leads down to the water. Children can often be seen treading warily down the steps in order to fill their buckets with fresh water to be taken home for cooking or washing. A reasonable through-flow ensures that the pools are generally clean and clear. The smaller pool is overlooked by a café, which sells overpriced drinks. The larger pool is overlooked by the arcade of a house built by the Dar El Bey. A tall palm tree also hangs over the water. The long-established tourist attraction of small boys making hair-raising leaps from the palm has temporarily halted, as the restorers' scaffolding now covers much of this *piscine*.

Other than the pools, there are few sights in Gafsa, although you could make a short walk to see the Grand Mosque and the Kasbah. Both are attractive in the fading sunlight of evening, but neither is worth writing home about.

The Central Interior

Kasserine

The 100 km journey from Gafsa to Kasserine is bleak and desolate. The bus makes few stops as it makes its way along Route 15. Table-topped mountains rise up in the distance, as the road crosses a plain of occasional palms and scrub vegetation. The aleppo pines which sometimes fringe the road are home to nests of orange caterpillars. These attract predatory shrikes. Look out for small bushes which are a spiny form of white pea. In less than 80 km, you come to Thelepte – the unimpressive remains of a Roman town. Join Route 17 for the 30 km run to Cillium. Kasserine then lies a couple of kilometres along Route 13.

Kasserine usually gets a roasting from the guide-books. Paris it certainly isn't, but even so, there are worse places to spend a day or two. There are a couple of reasonable restaurants on the central square, and an excellent supermarket (*magasin general*) on the main shopping street. The Hotel de la Paix is the best bet for central accommodation. 3500 dinars per person will get you a room with bidet and washbasin, with a bath and shower in easy reach. Despite good facilities and a convenient position close to the bus station, it remains a fairly characterless place in which to stay.

Just outside the town, on the Gafsa road, is the Hotel Cillium. This three-star hotel is very pleasant and serves excellent food. There are several Roman remains nearby, including a large arch near the piscines and a mausoleum by the side of the road leading into Kasserine.

A worthwhile excursion outside the town takes you beyond Kasserine on the Sbeitla road. After several kilometres there is a right turn, crossing a railway line that runs close to the main road. Tall prickly pear bushes abound here. The road winds off through the olive groves. After a few kilometres the mountains on the right become easily accessible. Their slopes are carpeted with dwarf and large juniper trees. A careful inspection of the ground reveals numerous marine fossils of bivalves and brachiopods (*Gryphaea*) among the limestone clitter. The general views from here are impressive, and black kites and great grey shrikes are a common sight in the sky.

Heading northwards from Kasserine, you are faced with two

obvious choices. The buses follow the 123 km stretch of Route 17 that leads to Le Kef. Route 5 then takes you 75 km north-eastwards, to Teboursouk and the ruins of Dougga. Alternatively, Route 13 heads east for the 40 km between Kasserine and Sbeitla. After driving northwards along Route 71 for 70 km, you can follow a minor road that cuts across to Maktar. 6 km north on Route 12, you take a right-hand turn on to Route 4, for the 35 km run to Siliana. Teboursouk lies about 50 km to the north, via Routes 73 and 18. Understandably, the latter route (which runs parallel to and west of the former) is only practical with your own transport.

The West – via Sbeitla and Siliana

Sbeitla

Sbeitla, 38 km from Kasserine, is famous for housing the excellent remains of a Roman town, Sufetula. The site lies to the left as you enter Sbeitla. The well-preserved Forum dominates the walks, paved roads and passages. The entrance fee is nominal with a much higher price to take photographs. As you walk towards the Forum, a group of buildings stand to the right. These are the baths, a theatre and a church. From here the main street takes you up to the Forum and to the group of churches beyond. The ground is littered with fragments of pots and tiles. During the springtime you may be the only visitor here.

Maktar

Two routes lead to Maktar from Sbeitla. The quickest is the MC71 that runs almost due north. The second is the MC77 which branches off Route 3 – the Sbeitla/Kairouan road. Maktar is in the centre of a remote mountain range, so the latter route is fairly slow, but quite breathtaking.

The northward route is faster, but it still passes through some beautiful scenery. The MC71 crosses the national Route 4. After this right-turn up into the mountains, it is 21 km to Maktar. The mountains can be seen through the eucalyptus trees to the east as you follow the MC71. They are hard-capped with horizontal bedding. Huge scree slopes descend to the plain below. Maktar seems to be built around a T-junction, but there is a noticeable lack of signposts. Turn right. (The left turning runs into a series of back-yards.) It is easy to become lost here. To the east of the town there is a roundabout near a Roman arch and some other remains. The road to Kairouan passes through the aleppo pine forests of Kesra. Rising over 1,000 m in height, these are very spectacular. Route 4 goes north through almost equally beautiful territory.

The road clings to the remote limestone mountains, occasionally passing through thick stands of pines. Stunted holm oak, holly oak, juniper and heathers all grow above the treeline. The blue globe flowers of *Globularia* emerge in spring from the spiny green growths in the rock. This is superb walking country, with fabulous panoramas from the summits. In winter and early spring it can get surprisingly chilly.

The road descends to Siliana. From there, the route north to Dougga is somewhat uneventful.

The East – via Le Kef

The bus ride from Kasserine to Le Kef takes 2½ hours. If you have your own vehicle, there are a couple of stops worth making en route. Leaving Kasserine, Route 17 makes its way across the rest of the barren steppe, before beginning a steady climb into the hills around Djebel Semmama. A little under 50 km from Kasserine, you come to Thala. At an altitude of over 1,000 m, this is a comfortable place to stop during the summer months. Other than admiring the

The limestone scenery around Maktar

scenery, there is not much to do in this small, hillside village, which is largely devoted to the processing of quarried marble.

A minor road 15 km further up Route 17 leads off to the left. In 20 km, this will bring you to the remains of Roman Haidra. A variety of ruins bear testament to the area's Roman, Vandal and Byzantine pasts. Classical scholars may like to take one of the tracks northwards towards the mountain of Jugurtha's Table. If the supposed stronghold of the Numidian king cannot bring the dimly remembered schoolday details of the Jugurthine Wars to life, nothing will.

Back on the main road, the town of Tadjerouine lies a little over 20 km to the north. At this point the fertile plain scenery gives way to the hills around Le Kef itself, which perches on the slope of Djebel Dyr, some 40 km further on.

Le Kef is a delightful town, in a spectacular setting. When unobscured by cloud, the view down to the plains and the hills beyond can be quite breathtaking. Breathtaking, in a different way, is the walk from the bus station (halfway up the hill) to the middle of the town. There are two obvious hotels in the centre. The Hotel de la Source is a little pricey, but has had good things said about it. The Auberge Hotel is, however, relatively cheap (2.500 dinars per person) and truly ghastly. Apparently in imminent danger of collapse, it is dirty and fly-infested. On our last visit, someone even knocked on the bedroom door at one o'clock in the morning, to ask for a cigarette. Compensations include the view from the bedroom windows and, well, that's it really!

The kasbah stands on the highest point of the hill, overlooking the rest of the town. It was strengthened and extended in the early nineteenth century, in response to a perceived threat to the region from Algeria. A Roman basilica (now a museum) stands in the square below the kasbah. Simply by walking through the narrow streets of Le Kef you will be rewarded with a succession of fascinating views. Behind a large domed mosque, you will find two small courtyards crammed with a jumble of stone Roman artifacts, carved with wheels and water pitchers in bas-relief.

The most impressive views over the plains are from the Avenue Bourguiba, which curves away from the square by the hotels. Making your way past tempting patisseries and splendidly colourful displays of fruit and vegetables, you will come upon the busy town market. Equipped with a peach or a cake, you can relax, sitting on the wall and gazing over the landscape spread out far below.

Teboursouk (the most convenient base for exploring the Roman town of Dougga) is to be found just under 70 km to the north-east, along Route 5. The bus takes 1½ hours, passing through attractive, hilly countryside on the way.

Much of this region is actively farmed. Cattle and sheep are left to graze in the fields bordering the road. The settlements on this stretch are mostly simple farming towns.

Teboursouk and the Ruins of Dougga

The bus from Le Kef leaves Route 5 and winds up into the centre of Teboursouk. This pretty farming town is the nearest settlement to Dougga. Unfortunately, there are no hotels in the town centre itself. The only place to stay is the Hotel Thugga, back down on the main road to Tunis. Do not bother to follow the road to the hotel, as a pathway leads straight down through the trees, almost halving the distance you have to walk. The path starts just opposite the junction in the town that is signposted for Dougga. At the bottom of the pathway, you only have to walk 100 m or so to the left, and you reach the driveway of the two-star hotel.

With en-suite bathroom, a twin-bedded room at the Thugga will cost 8.500 dinars per person, including breakfast. Unfortunately, there is nothing cheaper in the area.

To get to Dougga, you will have to return to the centre of Teboursouk, and then follow a winding road for 6 km. Although quite a haul, the scenery is ample compensation for the walk. The browns and greens of the valley beneath stretch far away into the distance. Alternatively, if you have your own vehicle, stop on Route 5, about 4 km before the Teboursouk turning. Rather than walking around the edge of the valley, you can then simply climb up the hill, to the north of the road. As you do so there is an impressive view of the remains, spread out on the slopes above.

If you approach from the Teboursouk road, there is a 1 dinar charge for access to the ruins. Guides will offer to show you round the ruins – certainly worth it if a group of you split the cost. Immediately on your right there is a large, semi-circular theatre. This is still used for performances, and the stage and vomitoria have thus been restored. The high bank of stone seating gives a beautiful panorama through the remaining columns behind the stage, and out to the valley beyond. An impromptu burst of Hamlet's soliloquy will graphically demonstrate the quality of the acoustics.

Roman ruins at Dougga

From the theatre, a delightful (and surprisingly winding) paved Roman street leads down to the Square of the Winds. A large circular dial is carved into the paving slabs, indicating the names and directions of the twelve winds. For example, at the southerly edge of the dial is the word 'Africus', which refers to the hot wind from the Sahara.

On the other side of the square is the Capitol. This huge temple has appeared on thousands of Tunisian Tourist Board posters. A set of steps lead up to four, grooved Corinthian columns. On top of these rest the architrave (beam) and the frieze. Finally, a vast, triangular pediment shows Emperor Antoninius being killed by an eagle. Through the columns, a rectangular arch leads into the inner chamber of the temple, where a 6 m statue of the god Jupiter once stood in an alcove. The edges of this chamber are piled with inscribed fragments from several of the town's buildings.

Looking over the valley from the Capitol, you can see the various contributions from the civilisations that have inhabited the area. Most obvious is the tower-like Punic mausoleum, that dates from around 300 BC. On a hill over to the west, the remains of a seventh century Byzantine fort can be made out. The next occupants were the Vandals, who appeared between one and two centuries later.

Walking down the hill from the Capitol, you pass through a

small square arch into what was the slave market. Scratches in the stone slabs nearby were used to enable camels to get a foothold in the wet. Around to the left are the Licinian Thermae. A tunnel leads down to the chamber where fires were lit to heat the water. The various chambers, each corresponding to a stage in the Roman bathing process, are remarkably well-preserved. It is fascinating to gaze around this part of Dougga, where the vast expanse of remains make it easy to imagine the bustling residential area that this once was.

Many birds nest among the ruins. Look out for the brightly coloured Moussier's redstart, hunting for insects. It is black above and red below.

Having looked around the city, there is a café just below the entrance where you can sit and enjoy a soft drink before beginning the trek back. (If possible, you should try to hitch a lift out here during the early afternoon, and then walk back during the cool hours of the evening. The colours of the valley are at their most beautiful at this time of day.)

In our next section, we describe a suggested route from Teboursouk to the far north of Tunisia. You can, however, make your way straight to Tunis from here. The buses stop here on their way from Le Kef. Be prepared to do without a seat. If you drive yourself, it is simply a question of following Route 5 for the 100 km to the capital. About 12 km along this road, look out for the impressive Byzantine fortress at Ain Tounga. The most attractive stop on the road, though, is Testour. Close to the river Mediorda, this town was built by settlers from Andalucia in the 1600s. If possible, try to pass through here on Friday. This is market day, as well as being the time when most of the townspeople assemble at the Grand Mosque.

The North Coast

The Cork Oak Forests of the Atlas

The MC75 from Teboursouk heads north-eastwards through a beautiful scenery of hills and valleys. The countryside becomes greener by the moment. Near the roadside and along the hedgerows are groups of long, dark, green, sword-like leaves growing from swollen tubers. These are asphodels, which flower in the spring. They produce a tall stem that repeatedly branches to hold white flowers, each with brown veins running through the petals. The asphodel is common around the north coast of Tunisia and grows to over a metre in height. In this region there is a gradual merging of African butterflies with European species. Hence we find varieties of painted lady and red admiral. The road curves round to Beja, but you should turn left at Bou Salem and head for Jendouba. This road winds its way through the hills. On the stretches where it straightens out, look out for low-flying hunting harriers.

The town of Jendouba has just one hotel, the Atlas. It is near the centre of the town. To reach it, you have to negotiate a confusing

The asphodel flower

one-way system. This is made all the more frustrating as the signs to the hotel point in the opposite direction to the traffic flow. It is preferable, however, to stay in the mountains near Ain Draham. This is especially so in the summer months, when the mountain area is much cooler. During the winter months it can be quite cold, but the hotels have central heating.

The route from Jendouba crosses the railway link from Algeria to the west. It is lined with squalid butchers' shops. Live animals are tethered outside the pink-walled huts. Only a few kilometres out of the town there is an unsignposted right-turning to Bulla Regia, an important Roman site. The GP17 is a good road which climbs steadily up into the cooler Atlas mountains. After about 20 km you cross a muddy river choked with oleanders and reeds. This area is also scattered with dense patches of eucalyptus. The plant life encourages butterflies and dragonflies.

Just beyond Fernana, the road begins to wind upwards into the hills, hemmed in by a dense forest of holm and cork oak. In addition, there are pines and Lusitanian heathers. This variety of tree heather is particularly abundant on the northern slopes of the hills. The steady climb of the road reaches almost 1,000 m. There are few higher points at this end of the Atlas range.

Progressing northwards from Jendouba, note that the soil colour changes from black to a sandstone-red. As a result of the high rainfall in this region, a reservoir has been built in the mountains. A track leads to the lake and the Beni M'Tir dam from a junction two-thirds of the way from Fernana to Ain Draham.

A short distance south of Ain Draham, the Hotel des Chenes is set in the midst of the forest. This old hunting lodge is fairly run-down with peeling paint and antiquated plumbing. It is, though, very comfortable, with a roaring log fire during the winter. Nine hundred metres above sea-level, it offers splendid views across the cork oaks. The Chenes is an ideal base from which to explore the forest. The Hotel Rihane is in Ain Draham itself. It is newer, but also more expensive. Hunting parties frequently use the hotel as a base for shooting wild boar.

Ain Draham is the main settlement in the Khroumir Forest. This vast wooded region stretches across the Atlas Mountains. The presence of the Algerian oak (*Quercus canariensis*) gives some idea of the extent of the forest. With a lobed edge to its large leaves, this semi-evergreen tree is reminiscent of the British oaks. Khroumir is a working forest, where most of the revenue is derived from cork. Bark is regularly stripped off the cork oak to a height of almost 3 m.

The cork oak forest near Ain Draham. The shrubs are heathers

This leaves a dark, red-brown trunk. Old bark supports considerable growths of epiphytes — Polyphody fern, and broad and filiose lichens. Ground flora is generally poor, because the trees are evergreen. There is more growth on the slopes, and in other areas where the trees thin out. Irises, asphodels and lillies all flower in the spring. The predominant shrub, growing by the roadside and under the oaks, is the Lusitanian heather (*Erica lusitanica*). This is very similar to the tree heather (*E. arborea*), which is found throughout the *maquis* vegetation of the Mediterranean and in the Khroumir Forest. The former species is distinguished by the long, pale pink corolla of petals, which give a distinct cylindrical flower. In young flowers, the buds are pink and the stigmas red. The Lusitanian heather grows up to 3 m in height whilst the tree heather can exceed 4 m.

On the northern edge of the Khroumir Forest, especially near the road, you will find the blue-leaved wattle (*Acacia cyanophylla*). In spring, their bright yellow globe flowers contrast beautifully with the rich brown trunks of the cork oaks.

As well as exhibiting an amazing change in vegetation, the mountain region is an interesting place for the ornithologist. From a woodland clearing on the upper edges of the valley, it is possible to see eagles and vultures soaring at the same level. Wild boar is not the only game animal to be found in the forest. Hare and foxes are commonplace and it is said that genets, wild-cats and jackals abound.

Ain Draham ('the source of silver') is only a few miles from the Algerian border. The road north to Tabarka goes through a smaller settlement called Babouch. It became infamous among conservationists as the place where the last lion and panther in Tunisia were shot. There a number of shops here, and a junction which leads to a dead end at Hammam Bourguiba. This hot spring area was so named because the erstwhile President was a frequent visitor. As well as the changes in the countryside, you will also notice a difference in building styles. The red-tiled roofs seem European in design. Wood carving is an important craft in the region. A wide range of carved animals and birds are sold from roadside stalls in the forest.

The marshy ground on the approach to Tabarka is home to numerous egrets, as well as the occasional stork.

The Coral Coast: Tabarka to Bizerte

This fertile part of Tunisia was the 'bread basket' of Rome two thousand years ago. The indented coastline stretches for 300 km from Tabarka, near the Algerian border, to Bizerte. The road is considerably shorter as it cuts inland to avoid the beaches. Fortunately, this also means that the coast remains wild and undisturbed. Only a few tracks, such as the ones to Cap Negro and Cap Serrat, are passable. These are badly signposted from the main road.

Snorkelling and scuba-diving off this coast is superb, as the coral reefs abound with marine life. This is especially true around Tabarka. Much of the reef area is not true coral, as one would find in hotter climates. The red 'coral' is a mixture of algae belonging to the genus *Lithophyllum*. They deposit calcium within their cells and thus produce a hard structure that looks like coral. In some areas the reef is several metres thick. Where it grows in folds, the crevices and gullies are inhabited by sea slugs, urchins and crustaceans. La Galite is a small island archipelago off the coast. It can be reached by boat from Bizerte. The remote location encourages seabirds and the Mediterranean seal. The latter is a protected species.

Tabarka is a pleasant town, with a market near the docks. The market sells a wealth of fruit and vegetables grown in this verdant

The green coast between Tabarka and Bizerte

valley. This is in stark contrast to the desert markets of the south.
The piles of carrots, oranges, chillis and peppers are a riot of colour.
Just to the east of the town, stone pines grow amidst sand dunes.
Egrets and storks stand by the roadside or glide overhead. The road
to Bizerte is 145 km long. Along this route, you will find that the
acacia karoo is a common plant. It has stout spines up to 10 cm in
length. The leaves suggest a cross between an acacia and a mimosa.
This species is a native of South Africa and has been cultivated for
hedges.

Leaving Nefta, you soon come upon a railway bridge. Just
beyond this, a track leads off to Cap Negro. The Bizerte route continues eastwards, but the main road veers to the south-east, via
Mateur. Heading for Bizerte, the unmetalled, stony track passes
through an expanse of delightful countryside. During spring and
early summer, a myriad of flowers transforms the lowland into a
blaze of colour. The singing skylarks, the darting groups of gold-
finches and the incessant buzz from the hive bees combine to create
an atmosphere of lush fertility. Eventually the track meets a cross-
roads – Bizerte 61 km, Mateur 45 km. Straight on, the MC51 leads
to Bizerte. This metalled road passes through an undulating landscape. Lake Ichceul comes into view 26 km before Bizerte on the
right.

Lake Ichceul

A short distance beyond Teskraia on the MC51 there is a junction with the MC57, which comes up from Mateur. A little further on, opposite some buildings on the left, a rough track leads down to the lake through pasture land. This gives good access to the upper lake. Continuing along the road, you come close to the lake, near some reed beds. If possible, however, it is worth taking some time to walk around the edge of the lake.

Lake Ichceul is a National Park. To the south a range of limestone hills provide a magnificent backdrop. In addition, they are important breeding sites for Egyptian vultures and Lanner falcons, as well as other important raptors. Moussier's redstart is a black bird with a white eye stripe and red sides to its tail. It is common in the scrubland around Ichceul and throughout northern Tunisia. These 50 sq. miles of water and marshland constitute one of the best wildfowling sites in the Mediterranean, next to the Camargue in France.

Ichceul is a permanent lake fed by six freshwater rivers. The proximity of the sea means that both the level and the salinity of the water vary considerably through the year. As too much variation

Lake Ichceul, which supports a bird population of 150,000

can be disastrous for the wildlife, a series of sluices are now used to maintain optimal conditions for the various species. In spring, the receding water level allows wild gladioli, ox-eye daisy and marigolds to flower in the wet meadows around the edge of the lake.

When the shallow lake warms up, this encourages invertebrates to breed amongst the fennel pondweed, grasses, saltmarsh plants and sea-club rushes. Both the flora and fauna help to support a bird population of 150,000. The list of species that can be seen here is very extensive. Egrets, herons, bitterns, flamingos and the rare purple gallinule feed around the margins. Waders such as stilts, pratincoles, godwits, avocets, redshank and little stints run along the edge. During the winter and spring, there are a surprising number of grey lag geese towards the western end of the lake. These are rarely seen in Africa. Other wildfowl, such as shoveller ducks, wigeon, pintail, teal, gadwall and pochard, form vast 'rafts' floating on the surface of the lake.

Lake Ichceul is a unique site that should be a part of any naturalist's itinerary.

Bizerte

The industrial town of Bizerte stands near Africa's northernmost point – Cap Blanc. It boasts a wide selection of hotels and a youth hostel. Some of the better-value hotels are slightly out of town, on the corniche that heads north to Cap Blanc. We recommend the Petit Mousse, on the edge of the beach. The accommodation is clean and the restaurant excellent.

En route southwards to Tunis, the road passes by the coastal area of Raf Raf. Although the tourist guides tend to enthusiastically extol its virtues, Raf Raf itself has little to offer, especially outside the main tourist season. Unless you are prepared to walk some distance from the built-up areas, it has a rather seedy atmosphere. The beach is narrow with large beds of eel grass growing offshore. Strong winds blow much of this on to the beach. Ras Djebel is a small town nearby. It is famous for its embroidery and for being the home of the Tunisian Lee Cooper jeans factory!

Closer to Tunis, you can explore the ancient site of Utica, a few kilometres off the main road. Around 1100 BC, this was one of the first Phoenician trading posts. There are numerous examples of punic pottery at the site. The museum here sports a 'Temporarily Closed' sign which is several years old. There are a number of artifacts outside, including a beautiful mosaic.

Tunis

As most standard guide-books provide a perfectly adequate description of Tunis, we shall keep ours intentionally brief.

Tunis is a remarkably friendly and welcoming capital. Its layout is manageable and unintimidating, and encapsulates more than any other Tunisian city the fusion of the French and native influences.

For much of Tunisia's early history, the town was in the shadow of Carthage, a few kilometres along the coast. It is now, though, the lively centre of Tunisia's political and commercial life.

The French New Town is built on a simple grid system. The Avenue Habib Bourguiba is its main artery, running from the edge of the Medina to the shore of the shallow Lake of Tunis. Lined with cafés, patisseries, restaurants, hotels, airline offices and banks, this is the focus of the city's life. It is easy to spend hours seated at one of the benches on the tree-shaded central promenade, watching the world go by, or reading the foreign-language newspapers that are sold from large stalls.

Near the lake, in the Place de l'Afrique, an imposing equestrian statue of Hammam Bourguiba gazes down his avenue. These statues are familiar throughout the country, built at great expense to boost the President's ego. Now he has been deposed, all except this statue and one in Monastir (his birthplace) are to be removed.

Just to the north of the Place de l'Afrique is Tunis's main Tourist Office. You can guarantee that, unless the information you require is in one of the three standard leaflets, the bored creatures on duty here will be of precious little help.

A series of smaller roads and avenues run away from the Avenue Habib Bourguiba at right-angles. Those to the south are far more lively than those to the north, with a wide range of restaurants, shops and hotels. Try to make time for a walk around the bustling food market on the corner of the Rue Charles de Gaulle and the Rue d'Allemagne.

From the Cathedral and the French Embassy westwards, the Avenue Habib Bourguiba becomes the Avenue de France. This leads to a stone archway – the Porte de France. The archway stands in the Place de la Victoire. This open space is the meeting point of Tunis's old and new towns. Making your way from here into the medina, it is almost like entering a new country. As one might expect, you will have to go some way into the network of narrow streets, before escaping the more obviously tourist-oriented area. The Rue Djemaa Zitounia, which runs between the Place de la Victoire and the Grand Mosque, is lined with shops selling colourful clothing, brasswork and carpets. Discreetly positioned Amex or Diner's Club signs suggest that these are no place to find a bargain. When you reach the colonnade of the mosque, it is best to take your time and wander randomly through the fascinating souks. One of the best times to explore the medina is early afternoon. The covered alleyways ensure that the heat is not too oppressive, while the time of day means that the same can be said for the tourist hawkers. Rather than launching into a high-pressure sales pitch, the stallholders are content to wish you 'Good afternoon' and return to their games of draughts, played with the lids of mineral-water bottles.

Being the capital city, it is understandable that accommodation is relatively expensive in Tunis. You may also have to try two or three places to get a room during the summer months. Generally speaking, the hotels are more expensive, and of higher quality, the further away from the medina you go. A good bet is the Hotel Splendid, on the Rue Mustapha M'Barek (leading south-east from the Place de la Victoire). A room here costs 4 dinars per person. The only drawbacks are the mosquitoes and the sweltering humidity at night.

Unfortunately, because of the marshland on the other side of the medina, these are problems that afflict the whole city. Once again, you are better off the further you are away from the medina.

Tunis is well-endowed with reasonable places to eat. One of the most pleasant is the Hotel Capitole Restaurant. The Table d'Hôte is staple stuff, but good value at 2.500 dinars. The restaurant is on the first floor and overlooks the Avenue Habib Bourguiba. Also in the centre of town, make sure you pop into the two main patisseries on the A.H.B. – the Patisserie Populaire and the Café/Patisserie Marignan. They both sell the wonderful *lait de poule* (chicken's milk). This thick, delicious drink consists of egg yolk, sugar, milk and a choice of strawberries, peaches or pears, all of which are mixed together in a blender.

Useful Addresses

Morocco

Moroccan National Tourist Office
174 Regent Street
LONDON W1

Algeria

Algerian National Tourist Office (O. N. A. T.)
25 Rue Khelifa Boukhalfa
ALGIERS
Algeria

Tunisia

Tunisian National Tourist Office
7a Stafford Street
LONDON W1

British Embassy
Place de la Victoire
Tunis

Tunisian Embassy
29 Prince's Gate
LONDON SW7

Index